THE MOUNTA
THE MOU

THE MOUNTAIN BEHIND THE MOUNTAIN

ASPECTS OF THE CELTIC TRADITION

Noel Dermot O'Donoghue

T&T CLARK
EDINBURGH

T&T CLARK LTD
59 GEORGE STREET
EDINBURGH EH2 2LQ
SCOTLAND

Copyright © T&T Clark Ltd, 1993

All rights reserved. No part of this publication may be reproduced, stored in a retrieval system, or transmitted, in any form or by any means, electronic, mechanical, photocopying, recording or otherwise, without the prior permission of T&T Clark Ltd.

ISBN 0 567 09652 1 HB
ISBN 0 567 29247 9 PB

British Library Cataloguing-in-Publication Data
A catalogue record for this book is available from the British Library

Typeset by Trinity Typesetting, Edinburgh
Printed and bound in Great Britain by Bookcraft, Avon

In memory of
'The Old People'
Of the hills of South-West Ireland
And the Western Isles of Scotland,
Who lived and loved
   and prayed and suffered —
And danced and sang:
With the winds of the hills,
And the flowers of the valleys;
With the voices of the birds
And the coming and going of
   the moon and the tides;
With the dance of the sunlight
   and the music of the rain…

CONTENTS

Acknowledgements	viii
Introduction	ix
1. The Celtic Imagination	1
2. The Chapel and the Mountain	7
3. The Mountain Behind the Mountain	29
4. The Pilgrimage to the 'City'	39
5. The Presence of God in the *Carmina Gadelica*	46
6. The Hidden Presences	59
7. Celtic Creation Spirituality	70
8. Cosmogenesis and the Celtic Imagination I	81
9. Cosmogenesis and the Celtic Imagination II	103
10. Memory and the Imaginal World: the 'Keening' Tradition	126
Index	139

ACKNOWLEDGEMENTS

The poem by Kathleen Raine in Chapter 3 is taken from *Kathleen Raine: Collected Poems 1935-1980* published by George Allen and Unwin (London), 1981.

The poem in Chapter 7 is taken from *Carmina Gadelica* by Alexander Carmichael published by the Scottish Academic Press (Edinburgh).

Chapter 7 is taken from a paper read to the Catholic Theological Association and published in *The Month,* November 1990.

INTRODUCTION

At the centre of all the following explorations is a gradually clarifying and expanding intimation or perception. This perception reveals a hidden world distinct from both the world of everyday observation and from that opened up by way of rational and reasonable thinking and contemplation. At first this world seems to vanish into the regions of fancy and imagination, forming a kind of penumbra attendant on the physical light of the eyes and the intellectual light of understanding and the world of ideas. *There*, it would seem, through the sciences of observation on the one hand and the theories of the philosophers on the other, whatever truth the human mind can find will be found. All else belongs to the regions of poetry and imagination, necessary perhaps in their own way, but to be firmly excluded from our relationship with the truly real if we are to remain sane and wise and 'balanced'. Yet what this book will be exploring is the possibility that there is a region or regions of reality which are discovered by way of an imaginative inner perception that is not simply *pro*jective but delicately and profoundly *re*ceptive, receptive of a world or worlds of reality normally concealed so as to give space and place to our faculties of observation and thinking.

In these explorations I am connecting this hidden 'imaginal' world with that marginalised and forgotten Celtic world which is now being in various ways rediscovered. But I have felt happy in this enterprise only because I am seeing it in close connection with the ambience and style of living and feeling in which I grew up on a mountain in the South of Ireland, so that I could test its validity and reality by my own memories of what was all around me in and on the mountain. It was by this criterion that I could judge the world of Alexander Carmichael's *Carmina Gadelica* as authentic, so that this world in turn could extend and deepen my connexion with my own roots. It seems remarkable that people so far apart as the folk of South Kerry in the extreme South-West of Ireland and the people of the Western and Northern Highlands and Islands of Scotland should have been so deeply united in their attitudes and in their particular style of Christianity, and also in their sense of the pre-Christian sacred and 'mystical'. Language, of course, has much to do with it, for they spoke what was and still is, in its remains, essentially the same Gaelic language, but with this went a common and to some extent peculiar perception of hidden worlds. This is common to most folk cultures, but it has and had in the Celtic world a special 'feel' or flavour which can only be called unique and cannot really be captured into the net of words, though one may perhaps meet it in the music and song that has come down to us like a far-off echo of distant seas and the cries of birds over Northern waters. C.S. Lewis, in the opening chapter of *Surprised By Joy*, talks of 'Northernness', but can only hint at what that names and touches. Jessica Powers perhaps best defines this quality by the very intensity of her seeking of an understanding of it.

> I ask and ask, but no one ever tells me
> What place we go when I meet Gaelic music
> And we are left a little while alone.

So, perhaps I should say that this present book comes from a kind of life-long listening to this Gaelic music heard first on my own mountain in Kerry and heard again, with new clarity and freshness, in the precious collection of prayers and poems transmitted by Alexander Carmichael. I am not concerned with anything else that may be attributed to, or plausibly derived from, Celtic culture or religion either by scholarship or romantic fancy. I speak only of what I have directly experienced. This can perhaps be seen as the explanation for the very personal, and even autobiographical, quality of parts of this book.

I have included the chapters on 'Cosmogenesis and the Celtic Tradition' after some hesitation. The vision of Pierre Tielhard de Chardin as it arises within the twentieth century scientific community seems indeed to present a world-view totally alien to the Celtic ways of looking at the cosmos, yet I am convinced that it is the age-old Celtic consciousness of the great wonder of God's creation that animates the soaring unifying images that are the wings of 'Teilhardism' and that have provoked the extreme reactions of some academics. On the other hand, I feel that Teilhardism needs to throw open a window into the Celtic spirit-world to find the completion of its own truth. I am also convinced that the people of the *Carmina Gadelica* and of South-West Ireland would have loved this visionary priest from the country of Vercingetorix, the last of the Celtic chieftains who challenged the might of Rome, and who lives on in that memory that is *Memoria Dei* and the place of meeting of the divine and human in men and women. Something of this has come up in the final chapter which looks briefly at the Irish 'keening' tradition.

This book brings together articles written at various times and for various occasions. I have retained the original format for the most part, for the book is, I feel, sufficiently held together by a constant developing unity of theme. I was quite young when I was told about the seven wonders of the world, and indeed I was proud to memorise them and repeat the list to anyone who would listen. It took me many years and many journeys and the reading of many books to discover that the greatest wonder of all is the wonder of the world itself, a wonder shining through the world of common day, shining through the mountain where the journey began.

1

THE CELTIC IMAGINATION

I

The well-known bronze figure of the dying Galatian expresses well the pathos and the tragedy of the invasion of the imaginative and exuberant Celtic tribal world by Roman imperialism in the first century BC. By the fourth century AD the Celtic tribes in the mainland of Europe were hammered into the ground by the Roman legions and the 'Barbarian' invasions. What was left of their power retreated to the fringes and headlands of Europe, to Britain and Ireland especially. . . . As a defeated race the Celts were ready to receive the religion of the cross and the resurrection. I do not want to press this point too far, but it was surely by a kind of miracle that the 'remnant' of the Celtic world in Britain and Ireland went out as Christian missionaries to the spiritual conquest of the barbarian conquerors of their Roman conquerors. The Celtic monks not only looked northwards but southwards also, towards the Alps and beyond, in that extraordinary explosion of missionary activity from the sixth to the tenth century.[1] Modern Europe and all that it stands for, from Charlemagne to the present day, rests squarely on the foundation of this spiritual and cultural energy. So it was that the destruction and marginalisation of

---

[1] See 'Irish Monks on the Continent' by Tomás O. Fiaich in *An Introduction to Irish Christianity* edited by J. P. Mackey. (T&T Clark, Edinburgh, 1989), pp. 101–139.

Celtic Europe by the Romans and the northern and Eastern tribes resulted in the spiritual reconquest of Europe and the building of the greatest material civilisation that our planet Earth has produced as far as our historical records testify. When the Celtic people of Britain and Ireland had done all this, had laid the foundations of our present world, it was again rolled back, overlaid, marginalised even further to the far-off islands and wild places of Ireland, Scotland, Wales, Cornwall and Brittany. Normans, Franks, Saxons and others rolled over them, pushed them back to the companionship of seals and seagulls at the world's end.

The part of this Celtic marginal world that I know best is Ireland, that is to say the western seaboard of Ireland stretching from Kinsale to Inishowen. Ireland managed to fight off the Danes in the early part of the eleventh century, but almost from then on there has been seven centuries of more or less increasing oppression, culminating in the holy terror of Cromwell and the various confiscations and 'plantations'. The history of the other Celtic marginal peoples has not been very different, a long dark night which is now showing the first faint tips of 'rosy-fingered dawn'. (The Homeric phrase is relevant, for it is in the Celtic consciousness especially that the spirit of ancient Greece has lived on.)

Already this century has seen a great missionary outgoing and out-flowing of Catholic Irish and Protestant Irish and Scots, men and women carrying the Christian good news to the ends of the earth. At the same time, almost in counterpoint to this, there has been the great literary achievement of 20th-century Ireland: Yeats, Joyce, Shaw, O'Casey and others.

There is enormous energy here, an energy that today shows itself in Scotland in a kind of literary and artistic renaissance. On the religious side there is the emergence of Iona as a centre of Christian pilgrimage and Christian witness. Everywhere we find Scottish men and women who are becoming conscious of their ancient heritage and who are, as is the Scottish way, wanting to do something about it. In Wales this awareness of a great heritage is even more intense, and of course it has been central to Irish consciousness for almost a century. There is also Brittany, Cornwall, Celtic Canada.... On the other hand, it seems that the mighty Christian civilisation which arose over a thousand years ago from that first outgoing of the Celtic missionaries who conquered the minds and hearts of those tribes who swept across Europe and left the Roman Empire in ruins; - it seems that this Christian civilisation is well on the way to exhaustion and the extinction of the human spirit by the forces of technology and materialism.

All the while, in Africa and Asia, new peoples are being conquered by European civilisation, and these people are looking for soul and spirit within the world which they have entered, and which has in many cases enslaved and corrupted them. . . .

In the light of all this, people are beginning to look again at that ancient Celtic world which, though it has been largely marginalised and humiliated, is nevertheless still full of that same creative life and spiritual resources from which Europe was born a thousand years ago. We look towards a millenium, not a millenium of ending but a millenium of new beginning. A new world can come, not by crude material conquest and racial pride but from a spiritual power that has been purified and strengthened through many centuries of oppression and humiliation. This resurrection is in the deepest sense a Christian resurrection after t he image of Jesus of Nazareth, the lamb that was slain and that rises in the glory of his wounds and stripes and thorn-crowned kingship. So it is that the symbol of this resurrection is the Celtic Cross where the sun of Easter shines through the dark icon of the crucifixion.[2]

[2]On the background of the Celtic Cross consult, cautiously, *Sun and Cross* by Jacob Streit, Floris Books, Edinburgh, 1984.

II

So much for the Celtic story, told here in very impressionistic terms, yet for all that, I would claim, essentially true. For the rest of this introduction I want to tell a little of my own story insofar as it is relevant to my general theme.

I was born more than seventy years ago in the south-west of Ireland in a thatch-roofed farmhouse on a mountain-side that looked across a river-valley towards the lakes of Killarney ten miles to the west: at sunset the valley sometimes looked like a great ship moving in a fiery sea towards a world of golden promise, as it might be Tir-na-nóg, the land of eternal youth. The mountain side sloped upwards to the breast-shaped peak which, with its companion, was called *Dá Keek Anainn*, the Paps of Dana or Anu, the mother-goddess of all the earth.

So it is that when I come to name the various attitudes and beliefs that came to me as together forming my Irish-Catholic heritage, the first is a sense of unity with nature, with the mountains and the rivers, the valleys and the lakes, the trees and bushes, the animals, the birds in the sky and trout and salmon in river and stream. This sense of unity with nature was at once peaceful and painful, including both a keen sense of life and a sharp sense of death.

This unity with nature was felt rather than consciously expressed, yet it was given imaginative and poetic presence in the names of places, for every field, hillock, rock and hollow had its own name. There was 'the meadow of fair grass' and 'the meadow of coarse grass', 'the gap of the horses' and 'the cliff of the cats'. These were all in Irish, though already in my time English names were coming in. One especially of those musical imaginative Irish-Gaelic names remains glowingly in my memory: *Eshkeen A Girray:* 'the little hollow of the hare'. The name is fresh and wild and full of the spirit of the hills in the morning.

So that is the first and most basic attitude that I absorbed as I grew up in this atmosphere, a sense of unity with nature and the elements, absorbed unconsciously rather than posited objectively. Allied to this was a sense of the unseen world. You might call it a belief in fairies, the *Leannawn Shee*, a mysterious region continuous with the world of the angels and 'the faithful departed', continuous, too, with the world of the *Banshee* and the restless spirits seeking light and peace.[3] It would be quite wrong to define or identify the realities of this world too concretely, but it was very real all the same. It is still real for me, having survived many years of formal education not only in literature and theology but also in philosophy and in science. It is for this reason that I find certain aspects of Rudolf Steiner's system extremely acceptable, and why I feel at home in centres like Iona and Findhorn where one is very close to this hidden world with all its beauty and danger.

The third attitude I have brought with me from my cradle in the hills of Dana is a sense of human immortality, a sense that we human beings come from afar and return to that region whence we came, all that is expressed so eloquently in William Wordsworth's *Ode on the Intimations of Immortality*. This attitude belongs in the first place to the discourse-world of intimation and imagination rather than that of philosophical demonstration, though, in fact, most of the admittedly great philosophers have accepted it as reasonable and even demonstrable. So it is that I have the greatest difficulty in understanding those who genuinely feel and believe that death is the end and that, in the words of a Roman poet, 'the one night awaits us all'. I can breathe freely only in the atmosphere of immortal spirit and the final transformation of nature and all that is within my own living, breathing, vulnerable human substance.

---

[3] See *The Fairy-Faith in Celtic Countries* by W. Y. Evans Wentz, Oxford University Press, 1911. Reprinted in 1977 by Colin Smythe, Gerrards Cross, Bucks., England with an introduction by Kathleen Raine.

The next basic attitude that can, I think, be traced back to my cradle in the immemorial hills is a love of learning and an appreciation of every kind of teaching and education, so much so that to me every teacher is a priestly figure, and in my own case I see my twenty five years of teaching as intimately part of my priesthood. In that very 'backward' hamlet in the hills where I grew up, we had very few books nor had we the money or the enterprise to acquire them. The 'old people' were, many of them, great story-tellers, and every place and event was given a kind of narrative context so that one had what is more precious and profound in the education of youth, an initiation into the mystery of wonder, so that one could breathe that pure air of the disclosure of truth which is, or should be, the aim of all teaching and all learning. Again this sense of wonder has never left me, and I pray that it never shall.

Allied to this is the love of words, of poetry and rhetoric, which I think is central to the Celtic mind and which, for all its openness to extravagance, is surely the life-blood of all real philosophy and theology.

But I leave this and many other attitudes which seemed to arise from my cradle in that ancient, forgotten, humiliated and oppressed world and seemed to cling still to the hills and valleys of Ireland. I freely admit that the values within these attitudes, perhaps even these attitudes themselves, have surrounded other cradles in other places and traditions. Yet I think that there is something that we should at all costs recover and rediscover before it has vanished forever from the earth. I have called this something the Celtic Imagination, at once a vision and a way of life. It has its shadows, like all human vision, and I have not looked at these here. But it has, I believe, enough light to help illuminate a future in which all other lights have begun to grow dim and to vanish into the dark.

2

THE CHAPEL AND THE MOUNTAIN

I

The primary environment of Christian theology as the understanding of the Christian message is the world of human truth and human love. The Christian message of new life and eternal salvation is not like a bolt from the blue but like a sunrise that takes its colours from earth and sky and sea. I am talking here of the spiritual landscape, the world of mind and heart into which the Christian message and the Christian vision come. More concretely, I shall be looking at the way in which the new religion of Christianity met the old Celtic religion of the Druids and their ancient wisdom, met the deepest aspirations of a people sitting in darkness yet awaiting the dawn and guided by the moon and the stars, guided indeed by that very worship of the sun which was, as St. Patrick showed, a figure of the true sun which is the eternal light become man.

St. Patrick is of course, a key figure both in history and legend and in imagination. We have all been given a clear and formidable image of this holy man who, clad in the secure mail of Christian righteousness, defeated the Druids and put an end to the old religion and all its works and pomps, including a large colony of snakes. He was the man who challenged the fires of the Druids by lighting the Christian Paschal fire on the Hill of Slane and did prodigies of penance on Croagh Patrick and at Lough Derg.

All this is legend. It belongs to a devotional and folk tradition that should be respected and that has left us with spiritually powerful and enriching images and symbols that belong surely to the ascetical and mystical heart of Irish Christianity. However, there is nothing at all about any of this in the writings in which Patrick tells us about himself and his mission. In these writings, the *Confession of Patrick* and the less important *Letter to the Soldiers of Coroticus*, we meet, not a powerful wonder-worker but a very vulnerable man, a man of many tears, a man deeply sensitive to the judgement of others, a man who mourns all his life long a friendship broken by betrayal, a man deeply sensitive to the needs of his women converts, and, it must be said, with a keen sense of their beauty and charm.

But I am not concerned here with presenting a portrait of Patrick. This I have done elsewhere.[4] What concerns me here is the way the Christian message of Patrick entered the spiritual environment of what is called Paganism. Paganism is a negative and dismissive word, but it is hard to find any word that would affirm what was positive and holy in the religious environment of pre-Christian Ireland. However one names it, this pre-Christian religious faith and practice had at its vital centre a deep and constant sense of an invisible world continuous with the visible world — sometimes indeed showing through it — and of a world of the dead which had its own quality of life. It was a consciousness, an invocation and a celebration of a hidden dimension that alone gives meaning to human longings and to that which is most specially and poignantly human, the tears of things, that great ocean of pathos which is the stuff of all our greatest poetry and music.[5]

---

[4]See *Aristocracy of Soul: St Patrick of Ireland*. A Michael Glazier Book, The Liturgical Press, Collegeville, Minnesota, 1988.
[5]See *Heaven in Ordinarie*. Edinburgh, T &T Clark, 1979, chapters 4 and 5 on *Pathos*.

Into this world Christianity came, the story of the little child who was God and who had to enter into the very depths of human sorrow, darkness, lostness and terror and to illuminate it and transform it. If Patrick came only with the message of the Resurrection, of a triumphant divine person, he would have but added another name to the pantheon of Celtic deities. And of course this is how many of the legends tell the story, as if a more mighty Lugh or Mananaan had descended on the Hill of Slane. When, however, you read Patrick's own story, you find it is the story of a slave-boy looking up with tear-stained countenance to the all-compassionate Father, a Father who weeps (as his son wept over Jerusalem) at the loss of his beautiful and holy world and the hearts of his children turned away from him. It is that most holy and solemn sacrament in which the eternal pathos of God meets the opening pathos of young manhood. There may have been Christians in Ireland before Patrick, but it was Patrick, the slave, who first brought the Good News of a God with a human heart, a God of tears who has over the dolorous and glorious centuries made Its abode with us. In a more general way, the Christian message came to the Celtic world as to a people defeated and enslaved. We need only read Julius Caesar's account of his campaign in Gaul (the *De Bello Gallico*, well-known to secondary school students of my generation) to see Roman pride and cruelty trampling over a proud and lively people. In a place called Gergovie near Clermont-Ferrand in central France is a large statue of Vercingetorix, the great and generous Celtic leader who gave himself up to the mercy of Caesar to save his people. This mercy consisted of incarceration for a year, after which he was dragged in triumph by his captors through the streets of Rome and then beheaded. I cannot help seeing Vercingetorix as a figure of the Suffering Servant described by Isaiah and totally and divinely fulfilled in Jesus of Nazareth. It was from this Christianity of a people in chains that Patrick came, from a family that had taken on something of the trappings of the conqueror yet that surely gave him a deep sense of affliction; and it was out of this affliction that his deep and total love of the Father arose, as also his sense of companionship with the Suffering Son of God and his understanding of the consoling Spirit. That he should have found in Ireland a welcoming environment for all this is part of what has been called by a French writer 'the miracle of Ireland'. That response has been immeasurably deepened not only through the ascetical and mystical centuries in which Ireland evangelised Europe but especially through the dark centuries of oppression and enslavement from which we are only now emerging.

II

The Christian message of God-become-man to redeem and transform mankind arose within Judaism as the fulfilment of Hebrew prophecy. So it is that the New Testament takes its terms and concepts largely from the Old Testament. But already Greek wisdom and Greek philosophical speculation were present in the later Books of the Old Testament and were part of the world-view of some of the New Testament writers, St. John especially. Greek philosophy and culture was the first ambience or environment into which Christianity came, and our theology is largely an amalgam of Hebrew and Greek ways of presenting the Christ-event and its shattering and transforming implications. This came not only through those early theologians who wrote in Greek — the Greek Fathers of the Church — but more especially through the greatest of the Latin Fathers, St. Augustine of Hippo, in the 4th – 5th century, who remained all his life, however reluctantly, a disciple of Plato. The Platonism of St. Augustine dominated Christian theology in the West until the rediscovery of Aristotle in the 13th century and the amazing synthesis of Hebrew and Greek thought in the theological system of St. Thomas Aquinas. This dominated Roman Catholic seminaries and universities up to Vatican II, and it is still very powerful and pervasive.

On the other hand, there is the Roman influence in which hierarchy and authority are supreme. This provides a wonderful harmony of order and discipline like a great army on the march where, ideally, no individual steps out of line. From this point of view, the way to be a good Catholic is to keep in step with the local priest, who keeps in step with the Bishop, who keeps in step with the Pope. As it has developed over the centuries, this Roman authoritarian approach does not reject the Greek tradition of speculation and scholarship but rather tames and domesticates it, deciding what is to be taught, laying down limits to free speculation, above all choosing safe and sound men as bishops and teachers. When it is tempered with kindness and compassion and a real sense of the Cross of Christ this kind of theology and practice provides a reasonably happy atmosphere for all except those who wish to think for themselves in a radical and challenging way.

As it was given and received by our Irish ancestors of the Early Christian centuries this vision was deeply influenced by Greek philosophy and Roman dogmatism, and these influences are still with us. But as it was received into this environment — Irish and, more generally, Celtic — the Christian Gospel was deeply influenced by something else, and this too is still with us. It is not easy to find a name for this something else. It was, and is, like the other two, an environment, a special quality of mind and heart, a special way of perceiving the human person and its ambience. You could use the word nature, and indeed this word in its original Latin form, *natura*, is at the centre of the greatest philosophical thinker to emerge from this tradition, John Scotus Eriugena, whose genius illuminates the intellectual darkness of the 9th century and heralded the dawn of medieval scholasticism.

Perhaps the best way to tune into this environment is to look at one of those ancient documents in which it is clearly and sharply expressed: the Hymn of St. Patrick variously called the Breastplate of St. Patrick or the Deer's Cry: this latter title based on a legend which in its own way points to the unity of man and nature. This great Christian hymn, though it was not (say the scholars) composed by Patrick himself, nevertheless dates to very early times, the 7th or 8th century, and is perfectly in tune with Patrick's own authentic writings. It has been translated many times, by, among others, James Clarence Mangan and Alfred Percival Graves, both poets of undeniable distinction; but it is best known in the translation of a certain Mrs Alexander: *I bind unto myself today/the strong might of the Trinity.* It can be found in this version in Church hymnaries of various denominations.

As one would expect, Mrs Alexander, translating the hymn for her Victorian contemporaries, gives it a Victorian feel, softening some of its ruggedness and glossing over some of its pre-Christian echoes. Yet, for all that, the spirit of the original survives and shows us a Christianity deeply coloured by a consciousness, a mental environment, quite different from that of either Hellenism or Romanism, especially in the pervasive and disconcerting presence of the natural world of the elements, the sights and sounds of earth and sea and sky, the celestial bodies and their influences, the human body in its physical presence and dimensions.

There is one stanza especially in which the Celtic nature world commingles with the Christian vision. In Mrs. Alexander's translation it goes as follows:

> I bind unto myself today
> the virtues of the starlit heaven,
> the glorious sun's life-giving ray,
> the whiteness of the moon at even
> the flashing of the lightning free,

the whirling wind's tempestuous shocks,
the stable earth, the deep salt sea
around the old eternal rocks.

Speaking of this stanza, Professor P. L. Henry, in *Saoithúilacht na Sean-Ghaeilge* says that it has 'the savour of pre-Christian religion',[6] and this is all the more clear when we pass from the sonorous Victorian version to the original in its literal sharpness, beauty and clarity:

For my shield this day I call:
Heaven's might
Sun's brightness,
Moon's whiteness,
Fire's glory,
Lightning's swiftness,
Wind's wildness,
Ocean's depth,
Earth's solidity,
Rock's immobility.

It should be noted that this prayer does not simply call on nature to 'bless the Lord' as in the *Benedicite* hymn taken from the Old Testament: *Bless the Lord all ye works of the Lord,* etc. What the Breastplate does is something else. It calls on all the elements to bless and protect human beings, as if there were something holy and powerful already present in the world of nature. And not only holy in some passive sense but living and responsive, just as the angels and saints, invoked elsewhere in the hymn, are living and responsive.

So it was that from the beginning and right to our day Celtic Christianity has been at home in the world of nature and taken the pre-Christian nature worship, including sun worship, into

[6] *Oifig an Solathaire.* Dublin, 1976, p. 135.

itself. When St. Patrick in his *Confession* tells us that Christ is the true sun he is not dismissing the natural sun as merely providing a metaphor for the shining glory and nurturing presence of Christ, though, of course, he does mean all this and more at the metaphorical level. But he does not *only* mean this, as is clear from the account, written many years after the event, of his terrifying awakening dream of the great rock that fell on him and paralysed him. All he could do was cry out in terror, and the word he used in his heart-cry was 'Helias, helias' which could echo Christ's death cry of '*Eli, Eli, lamma sabacthani*' ('my God, my God, why hast thou forsaken me') but could also be taken as the Greek *helios* meaning 'sun'. The words that follow, in Patrick's account, resolve this question by deepening the mystery. For the account goes on: 'In that moment I saw the sun rise in the heavens; and while I was crying out 'helias' with all my might behold the splendour of that sun fell upon me, and at once removed the weight from me. And I believe I was aided by Christ my Lord, and his Spirit was then crying out for me'.[7] Here the sun is not simply a metaphor or image of Christ but rather a medium through which He shines. That same sun which we see physically is but the outward appearance of that light which enlightens every man and woman, as St. John the Evangelist tells us. We are here in that region between spirit and matter which is sometimes called the 'imaginal world' and which is central to Celtic religion. I shall return to this. But, first, I want to look at an ancient custom which seems to have persisted all through the dark centuries of

---

[7]This passage is paragraph 20 of the best available edition of the *Confession,* that of R. P. C. Hanson, in *Sources Chrétiennes* (Paris, 1978). See p. 10 of the *Irish Messenger* edition (by J. F. X. O'Brien), Dublin, 1924. This is still in print and is sufficiently accurate for the ordinary reader. See Bishop Duffy's annotated edition. A translation will also be found in *Aristocracy of Soul* (note 4 above).

Ireland's subjugation and the near-extinction of the Gaelic culture, and has only died out in our own day, though many people still remember it from the days of their youth. It is the custom of going to see the sun rising on Easter morning with the expectation that it may move and dance as a kind of manifestation of this central mystery of the risen Christ.

III

So far I have been looking at the question of (Christian) theology and environment from the point of view of what I called spiritual environment, using the word spiritual in a wide sense as including cultural and intellectual environment. I have been looking at the origins of Christianity in Ireland and in the Celtic world generally, comparing the Celtic reception of the Christian message to that of Greece and Rome. Briefly, I have claimed that, just as Christianity became wedded to *logos* in Hellenism, and to authority and law in Romanism, it became wedded to nature and the natural world, in all its various levels and regions, in the Celtic world. There is no question here of hard and fast divisions but rather of basic and diffuse attitudes, distinguishable certainly, and sometimes in opposition, but by no means exclusive each of the others. Greek philosophy and Roman order and hierarchy entered deeply into Celtic Christianity, the former especially, but that had to leave room for that original sense of the presence of nature and its various reflections which were either ignored or marginalised in the Greek and Roman versions of Christianity.

At this point I want to change our time-focus from the far past to the present or immediate past and, more gradually, from the sphere of spiritual environment to that of physical environment. And I think that one way of doing this is to look closely at the custom of going to salute the sunrise on Easter Sunday morning. This custom was common in many if not most country parts of Ireland until quite recently. I know people who were brought up to this, and there may be people who still do it. But it has mostly disappeared, as have many similar customs and local pilgrimages, though these latter are in some places being revived. The Easter Sunrise custom extended from the southern tip of Ireland to the Northern Isles of Scotland, and it is from Scotland that the best and most sensitive description of this custom comes. It will be found in that best of all collections of traditional celtic hymns and blessings and customs, the *Carmina Gadelica* of Alexander Carmichael, published in five large volumes between 1900 and 1954 by the Scottish Academic Press.[8] Here is the account as given by Carmichael:

> The people say that the sun dances on this day in joy for a risen Saviour. Old Barbara Macphie at Dreimsdale saw this once, but only once, during her long life. And the good woman, of high natural intelligence, described in poetic language and with religious fervour what she saw or believed she saw from the summit of Benmore:
> 'The glorious gold-bright sun was after rising on the crests of the great hills, and it was changing colour —

---

[8] All five volumes of the *Carmina Gadelica* are available separately and as a set from the publishers. There have been various adaptations and selections made from the *Carmina*. The most notable adaptation is that of G. R. D. McLean, *Poems of the Western Highlanders*, SPCK, London, 1961. This is now out of print, but a selection of McLean's poetic renderings has been issued as a small paperback by Darton, Longman and Todd. The best selection of Carmichael's own translations is that made by Adam Bittleston, with a helpful introduction, published by Floris Books of 21 Napier Road, Edinburgh. This collection is entitled *The Sun Dances*, and is the best way in to the Carmichael collection. For the story of Barbara Macphie and the Easter sun see *Carmichael*, Vol. 2, p. 274, or *Bittleston*, p. 98. A full edition of Carmichael's English translation has been recently issued as a large paperback by Floris Books, (Edinburgh, 1992). Strangely, this edition omits Carmichael's story of the vision of Barbara Macphie.

green, purple, red, blood-red, white, intense white, and gold-white, like the glory of the God of the elements to the children of men. It was dancing up and down in exultation at the joyous resurrection of the beloved Saviour of victory.'

'To be thus privileged, a person must ascend to the top of the highest hill before sunrise, and believe that the God who makes the small blade of grass to grow is the same God who makes the large, massive sun to move.'

I do not want to enquire at the moment as to how far or in what sense this experience was inner vision or outer reality. Clearly, it is, in some sense a *given* experience; if it were merely imagined or called up Barbara Macphie would have called it up many times. But it happened to her once only, and unforgettably, in a way not unlike the sun-vision of Patrick's waking dream. What most of all concerns me here, however, is the deep intermingling or interfusion of the Christian vision and the world of nature, as we stand on the hill with Barbara awaiting the dawn. Our companions are the birds and the animals and the sharp air of the morning and the sleeping valleys below us.

As the stars close their shutters
and the dawn whitens hazily.

I quote from that very Celtic poet, Thomas Hardy, as on a Cornish hill he recalls a lost love that never really blossomed. Barbara Macphie no doubt had her lost human loves to mourn for, as we all have, but her vision and her faith looked outwards and upwards. She did not expect a miracle, but she carried with her a sense of the God of wonder and surprises 'who makes the small blade of grass to grow and the large massive sun to move'.

In the tradition to which Barbara belonged, this attitude of total involvement in nature as a place of prayer and divine presence did not wait upon special occasions such as Easter Sunday; it was always there, not only in special events such as birth and death and marriage, in times of joy and catastrophe, but in all the routines of life: daily, weekly, monthly, yearly. In Carmichael's collection we find a hymn long or short for every occasion, and a whole sheaf of hymns and invocations for rising in the morning and lying down at night. These latter are a special feature of Celtic spirituality, as is clear from Douglas Hyde's *Religious Songs of Connaught*.[9] Perhaps I should say here that for me Douglas Hyde has done more than anyone to preserve and recover this tradition. He ranks with Carmichael in his dedication to the task, though it must be admitted that there is nothing in our Irish collections to rival the Carmichael collection for freshness, power, and the welding together of physical and social environment with Christian faith and practice. On the other hand, no Irish reader who knows the Irish past can fail to recognise it everywhere in Carmichael's pages. What I see when I look back in time and look around me at the unchanging hills and valleys and 'springs' and lakes and rivers among which I grew up, and which formed and still form the matrix or ground of my religious and cultural consciousness, is something truly rich and strange. I lived high up on the western slopes of the Paps of Ana or Dana, *Da Keek Anainn*, or *Keeka Danainn*, and ancient shrine of the Mother-God, and down in the valley beside the River Flesk was St. Agatha's Church or chapel where I was baptised in what Carmichael's people called '*uisge na brigh*, 'the water of meaning'. It seemed at first that God was there, in that chapel, with its black-suited priests, yet as I look back it is clear to me that for my opening imagination God was also on the mountain

---

[9] Dublin: M. H. Gill; London: T. Fisher, Unwin. My copy has no date, but probably dates from early in the 20th century. It is long out of print, but it may have been reprinted, for all I know.

and spoke to me and my people in a thousand ways, in dawn and sunset, in the sun, moon and stars, in the changing seasons and the changing weathers. Part of this was relevant to the church in the valley and its priests, but the greater part of it lay wide open to the sky, and had various dwellings in the secret places of the hills.

One yearly ritual will serve as an example and a symbol of the religion of the mountain: the Midsummer bonfire, or the Bonfire on St. John's Eve. My own memory of this is exclusively connected with my father, who, until his last illness and death in 1946, would go towards some part of the mountain where there was what we called *Brosna*, the whitened remains of furze burned in former years, and set it alight until it passed into the new furze and spread some distance along the mountain. Nobody tried to stop my father doing this, yet as far as I remember he received no encouragement from the rest of the family nor from the neighbours. He would say each year something like: 'We must keep up the old customs' or 'We must not let the old customs die'. It all happened on St. John's Eve, but the church down in the valley made nothing whatever of this occasions. Neither was St. John (the Baptist) particularly honoured or invoked in the lighting of the fire. It had to do rather with a pre-Christian commemoration of Midsummer Night. It was in this sense that it was 'an old custom', and I feel sure, looking back, that this was what my father meant. He went regularly to Sunday Mass in the church down in the valley, yet the deepest part of his being met with God in the ancient way, and when I last visited him before his death, when his mind was 'wandering', he spoke of fishing for trout and salmon in the mountain streams and in the River Flesk down in the valley. His soul's journey to the everlasting hills must surely have been by way of the Hills of Dana.

As far as I know, the St. John's fires are no longer lighted along the hills though no doubt the custom lives on elsewhere;

it continues, I am told, in the Massif Central in France, and people still go up to the Puy de Dome to light a great fire on St. John's Night (*les feux de la Saint Jean*) and await the dawn. This is the country of Teilhard de Chardin, a man of Celtic imagination, the place in which that Vercingetorix mentioned already, the last of the Gallic chieftains, is commemorated by a great statue on the hill of Gergovie, where Celtic France made its last stand against the Roman legions.

There is another remembered custom which served as a link between the mountain and the chapel — the visit to what was called 'the City' on the first Sunday of May. The City is today no more than a place of ancient, very ancient, memories; originally, it seems, it was a castle or citadel associated with a man or woman called *Crobh Dearg* or 'Red Hand' who stands ambiguously at the threshold of Christianity. It is also a Marian Shrine, with a well and a statue of the wayside Madonna, and people still come to the place on the first Sunday in May, and at other times, when Mass is offered and the Rosary recited. It is a quiet place under the shadow of *Da Keek Anainn*, and it is surely a place where the old religion of nature reaches out to the religion of supernature and the Christian mysteries. I shall return to this in chapter 4.

Now, a certain connection with nature and the changing seasons is present in all Christian communities everywhere. There are, or were, 'Ember Days' and Harvest Festivals, and various invocations and blessings on people and their work: this especially in agricultural communities, where the course of the seasons and course of the liturgical cycle tend to meet at various points. Moreover, the Psalms and other texts of worship tell of the glory of God in creation. All this, and more, is deeply and indelibly present in the Christian doctrine of creation. But the tension and polarity which I have localised in the chapel with the mountain rising above it is much more than this. For the Celtic religious consciousness, Christian as well as pre-Christian, creation does not merely show forth God's glory or enter into rites and festivities. Creation, the world of nature, has its own power, its own presence, its own mystery, its own voices. One calls out to it as did my father when he was dying, as I will too perhaps some day in my own way. This does not at all mean that Christ is forgotten or the need for the sacramental Christian community in its ministers and in its prayers. Rather does it mean that the Word through which all things were made is first and always present as creative, and only consequently present as redemptive. Christ crucified is present not only in the ever-renewed sacrifice of the Mass but in the bread and meat we eat — in the pig slain and hanging cruciform in the kitchen, as well as in the lamb and the hens and ducks and geese, or the hares and rabbits taken from the hills and uplands. In all this the Celtic way reaches back and reaches out behind and beyond Christianity, not only to tribal and aboriginal religions, but also to the Muslim world and Hindu world. I do not want to develop this theme here, but rather to look briefly at what I see as the key, or one main key, to the Celtic understanding of nature, and of its relation to the Christian mystery.

IV

What is this key that will open for us in our time and place the door into that ancient world of living and companionable nature? Is it a kind of belief or a kind of imagination? Is it that our mothers and fathers of the days of old believed more strongly than we do in the presence of God and the angels and the living dead, in the world of the sun and the stars, the wind and the rain, the rivers and the mountains? Or was it rather that they had a simple child-like imagination which peopled the world with the creations of their own minds, 'giving', as the poet says, 'to airy nothing a local habitation and a name'. All this is true, but this is not yet the key that will open the door for us into that enchanted country. No, the key lies in a kind of perception that is indeed close to imagination and is intertwined with belief, but is, nonetheless, as the Americans say, something else again. When these people saw the sun dancing, or the bright angels near them, or the *leannawn shee*, the fairy folk, passing by, they were indeed using their imagination, personal and traditional; they were also expressing a kind of religious belief that was connected, on the one side, with Druidism and, on the other, with Christianity. But beyond and beside all this they had a kind of vision that saw *into* nature, that discerned in and through and around it a real sphere of living presences, at once physical and spiritual, having physical shapes and colours but not held or contained by the conditions of the stable and yet corruptible everyday world. The sun that silvered and shook and threw out various colours was not/is not the sun of the astronomers nor of common observation; rather it is the eternal sun within the sun, the eternal living glory within what is after all a mere dead radiation of energy. Yet how can these rays give life, or at least nurture it and make it possible, unless they have somehow life in themselves?

The conception of a region of reality at once objective and physical — actually *there* and not just projected or imagined in the ordinary sense — and yet not subject to decay or death, and in that sense spiritual, is by no means a novel conception, nor is it without a place in Christian theology. It will be found for instance, in St. Augustine's doctrine of the glorified body as set forth in his treatise on *Genesis*.[10] it is sometimes, especially in the Muslim Sufi tradition, called 'the imaginal world' *(mundus imaginalis)*, because it is open to the imagination, not however the imagination as projective and fictive or creative but the

---

[10]See G. Watson: 'Imagination and Religion in Classical Thought' in J. P. Mackey (ed.) *Religious Imagination*, Edinburgh University Press: Edinburgh, 1986. On the literature on 'Imaginal' reality see note 37 below.

imagination as a faculty of perception, a faculty that perceives what is really there, though it comes, like all perception, not only as a pure datum, something given, but as a fruitful marriage of what is in the mind and what is outside it. It is in this sense that William Wordsworth describes ordinary perception as opening up 'the mighty world of eye and ear/both what they half create and what perceive'. The world of imaginal perception is likewise, yet in its own special way, a living union of the mind and the external world. 'The fairies dancing under the moon' may be really there, yet the poet (Yeats) will see them in his own way, as Barbara Macphie will see them in *her* way. In either case there has to be a kind of deep attunement not at all available at will.

It was by people thus attuned to this inner world — a world at once physical and spiritual — that the New Testament, and indeed the whole Bible, was written. The Gospels are full of beings called angels or messengers, who are quite physical inasmuch as they can be seen and heard, and have a human form and vesture. They are especially present at the birth and Resurrection of Jesus, and, as we can see from the Acts of the Apostles, they are very much present among the first Christians. It is because we have lost the faculty of attunement to the region these beings inhabit that we are all too easily persuaded by certain scholars that these beings are no more than imaginary and mythical.

The spirit-worlds of Celtic folklore belong to the same general region as that of the angels and demons of the New Testament. Sometimes imagination has gone free and unchecked in the stories that are told of this region, but there is no reason, if one believes in a Christian spirit region, to reject out of hand this fairy-faith of our ancestors. The fairy-folk have their home in what Kathleen Raine calls 'the mountain behind the mountain', and sometimes that region becomes visible and generally perceptible, as the sun within the sun sometimes speaks to those who are attuned to it.

The Christian faith gives its true centre to all this, yet in turn the spirit-world gives its natural clothing to the Christian faith. The chapel in the valley and the mountain of the ancient mysteries and the *leannawn shee* belong together. In all this the generations meet and mingle. We are with the dead, and the dead are with us. Recently a friend of mine — I will call him Donal — who was born under the Paps of Dana, came to a little field or 'haggart' in the hills, where he felt and heard the dead of his own family all around him, full of joy and excitement. Donal is a very responsible and truthful man holding a senior position in the Irish Civil Service. I do not doubt what he told me, nor do I doubt that the mountains, and the elements as far as the farthest stars, are full of the great spirits and the little spirits in the vast hierarchies that inhabit the world of nature.

V

As I stand on the mountainside and look down on the valley I am looking down not only on the chapel or church but also on the churchyard, the place of burial, the place of death. The churchyard, where my father lies and my mother, in their mortal remains, and the generations from which they came, is a peaceful and, in a real sense, a consoling place. This is the elemental earth from which I came, as they, my forefathers and mothers, came and to which I too shall return. In a sense these people are not where their bones lie; they are elsewhere, as I too shall be as they place my remains in the element of the earth or the element of fire. Yet the funeral rite speaks of the resurrection of the body as if the whole person somehow awaited resurrection here in this place. There is an ambiguity here that Christian theology, from the time of St. Augustine until today, has never quite resolved. Are the dead alive in another region, or do they somehow, somewhere *await* an awakening? Are they still somehow part of nature, or do they dwell in a spirit-world which may be near to us but is yet of a totally different substance? Are the men and women who walked the hills of Dana, and laboured in its fields and uplands, now without any presence in this place, now unremembering and unconcerned? Little of nothing is said about this within the hallowed walls of the chapel in the valley beside the river, though the pastors and preachers who come and go speak with one voice of the sure hope of a happy resurrection for those who in any sense die in the friendship of the Lord, and for the others there is the hope of mercy and purifying fires. But it all seems very far away, as the world of the rain and wind and sunshine seems very far away from the world of death.

Yet both the folk-consciousness and, at times, the poetic consciousness have another point of view which gives a kind of voice to the mountain. There are traditional phrases such as 'the good dead in the green hills' or 'she is gone to her people'; there are the many stories of the dead who variously disturb or console the living. A long time ago a Killarney writer named Seamus de Faoite, who grew up with me, wrote a one-act play called 'The Crake in the Meadow' telling of the death of an old man who lived in a kind of total openness to nature; death did not take him away, for he was still there with the crake in the meadow. So, too, Lord Byron, remembering his Scottish ancestry in a wild Highland place, says:

> Clouds there encircle the forms of our fathers
> They dwell in the tempests of dark Lochnagar.

We are here in the worlds of folk imagination and poetic imagination — each legitimate in its way — but surely having nothing to do with sober doctrine and solid theology. They belong to the world of the mountain and the pagan faith superseded by Christianity. Yet, if we take theology as represented by the man who is arguably the greatest Catholic theologian of our time, a very original man who yet stood firmly within the limits of orthodoxy, we find a surprising consonance between the two worlds. I am speaking of Karl Rahner, whose greatest merit perhaps is that he explored questions which most theologians sidestep more or less adroitly. In his book *On the Theology of Death* he has some interesting things to say. We cannot, he says, rule out the possibility that 'in death the relationship which we have with the world is not abolished, but is rather, for the first time, completed'. By death the soul becomes 'not a-cosmic but all-cosmic', that is to say not outside or outwith the world of nature but within it.[11] One might say that instead of experiencing nature from outside, we begin to experience it from within, as it issued from its creative source.

Rahner does not try — perhaps does not dare — to draw out the concrete implications of his theology of life after death, but I would suggest that the 'haggart experience' of my cousin Donal is in tune with this theology. What Rahner asserts in abstract theological language Donal tells us in the fresh and direct language of experience.

In 'the haggart experience' we are in the traditional world of the Irish storyteller. I remember well sitting by the fire as a little boy and listening to Donal's grandfather telling strange stories of the living and the dead. Looking back I can see that the location or ambience of all these stories was that inner 'imaginal' world shining through the world of physical nature, the world of the fairy-folk and the heavenly host in which those who had died from amongst us were very much alive. If you read Rahner carefully, you will find that, behind the wrappings of his theological abstractions, he is talking of a very present, strangely

---

[11] *Zür Theologie des Todes*, Herder: Friburg, 1961. Translated by C. H. Henkey (London, 1961) with an *Imprimatur* from the Diocese of Westminster. This means, we are told, that 'the book is considered to be free from doctrinal or moral error'. See pp. 27 to 34 of the English translation for the passages quoted in the text.

palpable spirit-world. For he brings in the traditional Christian doctrine of the angels on the one hand, and on the other what he calls 'the modern doctrine of life-entelechies and their relationship to matter' (p. 29). These latter are surely the spirit-beings sometimes called astral or etheric entities, and known familiarly in the Irish folk-tradition as the *leannawn shee* or 'the little people'. We are, of course, in a region that is not only accessible to folk-perception but vividly decorated by folk-imagination; yet the more or less happy extravagances of the latter must not blind us to the objective reality of the former. The mountain sacred to Dana is, like Prospero's island, full of voices, full of presences, and my father's liturgy of the fires of St. John, *les feux de la Saint Jean,* at Midsummer, is an acceptance of a threshold into the unseen, the *invisibilia* of the Nicene Creed, and of what lies dimly glimpsed, beyond the threshold of common perception. It is perhaps significant that the recent happenings at Medjugorje, part imaginary it would seem and part imaginal, began on the feast of St. John, Midsummer Christmas, the time of midsummer dreams and visions, the time of the light shining across the threshold of the invisible world.

In all this the mountain is speaking, but here, exceptionally, the chapel in the valley is listening and learning, for the priest cannot but listen to the theologian, however reluctantly. On the other hand, the chapel has something of supreme importance to say to the mountain, something for which the mountain has been waiting since it began to come forth from chaos at the beginning of creation. For the mountain and all its spirit inhabitants are held in a kind of captivity by the Adversary, Satan, the Lord of Death and Annihilation, and it is only through a divine principle of life that it can be released from this bondage and become truly itself. St. John the Baptist was, and is, the herald of this divine coming in human, vulnerable flesh, born of the woman who is at once Dana and Mary of

Mount Carmel, the Virgin of Nazareth. Through Jesus-Saviour, the anointed one, crucified and risen, a new principle of transformation and resurrection has entered the cosmos. 'The good dead in the green hills' have entered into this transformation, yet they are working constantly for the transformation of nature, the breaking of that ancient spell, the release of the cosmos from the fallen angels and archangels who may well at the end become part of that final glory. St. Paul, in chapter 8 of his *Letter to the Romans*, puts it all beautifully and mysteriously:

> I reckon that the suffering we now endure bear no
> comparison with the splendour, as yet unrevealed,
> which is in store for us. For all created nature waits
> on tiptoe of expectation for God's sons and daughters
> to be revealed because nature itself is to be freed
> from the shackles of mortality and enter into the liberty
> and splendour of the sons of God.

In the final glory the church and the mountain are one, and a new world begins. The Christian vision has found its total ambience and environment in a transformed world of nature.

3

THE MOUNTAIN BEHIND THE MOUNTAIN

I

I take this title from a poem by Kathleen Raine, poet in our day of the Celtic Tradition, and I want to quote this poem in full. It is called 'The Wilderness', but there is question of a wilderness that is awaiting a new burgeoning and blossoming.

> I came too late to the hills. They were swept bare
> Winters before I was born of song and story,
> Of spell or speech with power of oracle or invocation,
>
> The great ash long dead by a roofless house, its branches rotten
> The voice of the crows an inarticulate cry,
> And from the wells and spring s the holy water ebbed away.
>
> A child I ran in the wind on a withered moor
> Crying out after those great presences who were not there,
> Long lost in the forgetfulness of the forgotten.
>
> Only the archaic forms themselves could tell
> In sacred speech of hoodie on gray stone, or hawk in air,
> Of Eden where the lonely rowan bends over the dark pool.
>
> Yet I have glimpsed the bright mountain behind the mountain,
> Knowledge under the leaves, tasted the bitter berries red,
> Drunk cold water and clear from an inexhaustible hidden fountain.[12]

[12]Collected Poems, London: Allen and Unwin, 1981, p. 107.

The mountain behind or within the mountain is not the perfect or ideal mountain in some Platonic sense. Neither is it that mythical Mount of Parnassus on which the Muses dwell. Nor yet is it the Holy Mountain in which God reveals himself in theophany or transfiguration. Each of these mountains belongs to its own mind-set, its own world of imagination. The mountain of that kind of Celtic tradition to which Kathleen Raine belongs, and which nurtured the people from which I came, is neither an ideal nor a mythical mountain, nor is it exactly a holy or sacred mountain in the sense of a mountain made sacred by theophany or transfiguration. No, it is very ordinary, very physical, very material mountain, a place of sheep and kine, of peat, and of streams that one might fish in or bathe in on a summer's day. It is an elemental mountain, of earth and air and water and fire, of sun and moon and wind and rain. What makes it special for me and for the people from which I come is that it is a place of Presence and a place of presences. Only those who can perceive this in its ordinariness can encounter the mountain behind the mountain.

For the Celtic tradition, as for other primal traditions such as the Amerindian and the Australian, the mountain is alive as all nature is alive. From the worm under the ground to the lark and the eagle that inhabit the sky and the high places there is the one life everywhere, ever renewing itself, so that creation rests on procreation, and death and birth belong together. One understands this, not by thinking it, but *by living it as a thinking being*. It is in this way that much is understood by primal people, not by thinking things out intellectually but by *living* things as thinking and feeling beings. Thematic and systematic thought may close the doors of perception. Primal perception, for all its elemental realism, leaves those doors open, or at least ajar, so that the light of imagination, of that upward imagination of which Plotinus speaks, what George MacDonald names 'the wise imagination', may shine through and illuminate, for a moment or as a constancy, the mountain behind the mountain.

We relate to the world around us by the inner light of perception; indeed, there is a sense in which this light creates the world around us. Yet this light is interfused with the light of intelligence by which we variously pass judgment on experience. If we stop at this point we do indeed see the mountain and all its dimensions, all its fauna and flora, all its possibilities. We may even carry out a survey of the mountain, measuring it, assessing its fertility and possibilities of development. We can build a city on it, raise up towers and palaces and places of worship. As children of a technological age we can bring in cranes and bulldozers and every kind of machine, to build a great city on and around the mountain. We have thus made good use of the two lights that illuminate our knowing and doing. But we have missed the light of imagination, and we have had no vision at all of the mountain behind the mountain, the mountain from which flow the wellsprings of Creation. Our city, little or great, is not a sacred city made for man and God to dwell in, but merely a secular city without an eternal dimension, without any hope that God's holy angels may dwell therein.

II

What do I mean by the light of imagination, and what kind of reality does it reveal? This question, let us note, comes to be asked in the light of intelligence (source of all meaning), and insinuates that the criterion of reality is to be found in the light of perception and nowhere else. But the light of imagination can only find room for itself and what it reveals by challenging both the one and the other. To the senses it says: listen to the Presence, feel it, touch it, breathe it in. To the intellect it says: open up beyond the heavy material world to a Presence and presences that refuse to be controlled by your limiting categories, a Presence that you are longing to encounter and affirm, for it enriches and completes the meaning, the *rationale*, of creation.

This Presence is given a name in the Celtic tradition: the King of the Elements or the King of Creation — *Righ na nDúl* (ree na dool). So it is named in the *Carmina Gadelica* of Alexander Carmichael, where it sometimes takes the form of a triadic doxology, according to a sense of threeness that antedates all news of the Trinity.

No anxiety can be ours
The God of the Elements
The King of the Elements
The Spirit of the Elements
Close over us
Eternally.

But what of the presences? How do we encounter them? Are they creatures or figments of folk-imagination, or do they represent a whole world of entities that now at the end of the second Christian millennium are, so to speak, awaiting our recognition, offering their companionship?

In order to face these questions it is necessary to make some distinctions.

First it is necessary to distinguish between the imaginary and the imaginal. An imaginary being or world is created by our free faculty of imagination. To this belongs the fantasy worlds of George MacDonald, C. S. Lewis or J. R. R. Tolkien, the world of fictional *beings* and environments, and not simply, as in fiction generally, a world of fictional *events* and perhaps a strong fictional atmosphere, as with Thomas Hardy or P. G. Wodehouse. These fantasy worlds do not seriously pretend to exist as in any real sense continuous with our everyday existence. The imaginal world, the *mundus imaginalis*, on the other hand, does claim precisely this: that it is a continuation or extension of the world of everyday perception. There is more to be seen than is revealed to ordinary vision in the light of common day, a world waiting to be found that does not impose or force itself on us, a world that is at the very centre of physical creation as it comes forth from the source.

A second distinction that has to be made is that between private and shared experience, or perhaps more accurately between the private and shared aspects of experience. My vision of the other mountain, imaginary or imaginal, may be a private and personal experience which I may indeed share with others by telling them about it, but which, whether the others accept it as imaginal or imaginary, remains within the borders of my own experience. Or, on the other hand, my vision of the other mountain and its presences may arise within a tradition to which I find I belong by an affinity that may be, so to speak, in the blood or in the soul, that is to say, either racial or universally human.

A third distinction is that between the evidential and the intimational. The evidential is a matter of what Americans call 'hard-nosed facts' and involves the kind of investigation that would be undertaken by a prospector for gold or copper as he looked at the mountain. The intimational cannot be submitted to this kind of proof, for it has to do with matters that do not belong to the sphere of physical measurement. Wordsworth had intimations of the reality of another world by way of certain half-remembered childhood experiences; T.S. Eliot had intimations as he looked at the dreary London landscape of 'an infinitely gentle, infinitely suffering thing'; Patrick Kavanagh, an exile in London, thought of a scene from his boyhood and felt the God of Imagination 'waking in a silent bog'. In a pragmatic sense hard-nosed facts have noses as hard as ever, and our technology works better than ever, but those scientists who have had the temerity to look at the reality-base of it all might as well have been following Wandering Angus with Yeats through 'hollow lands and hilly lands'. To put it in another way, basically what I am saying is that those clever people who are digging up Croagh Patrick, the ancient sacred mountain in the West of Ireland, searching for gold or whatever, are less, not more, in touch with reality than the pilgrims who are led up that mountain by an ancient sense of Presence and presences. After all, Kathleen Raine, who has been our guide to the mountain behind the mountain, began her search for understanding with a botany degree from Cambridge, and came to realise that reality was elsewhere.

Let me return to the question: *What are these presences?* in the light of these distinctions. First, they belong to that imaginal world that opens up beyond the doors of everyday perception. Secondly, they are seen or sensed within an ancient tradition. And, finally, they belong to the order of intimation rather than the order of everyday evidence.

There is one quality especially which distinguishes imaginal from ordinary sense perception. It is this. The more sharply and carefully one tries to define, focus and describe what comes to us through the sense organs, the more we deepen and enrich our experience. This involves a kind of control of our environment by which we become more firmly situated within it and more competent in manipulating it. In the case of the imaginal world, however, we gain nothing by applying this controlling, defining method to it. We must allow it to come and go in its own way, to preserve its own reticence and delicacy, to exercise a certain gentle control over our avid desire for knowledge as a possession, to calm and refresh the spirit rather than to send it into a spiral of questioning. We have been beckoned across the threshold of a sanctuary where we must put off our shoes and tread very gently indeed. It is painful for any genuine visionary to be asked to bring this delicate experience into the world of scientific tests and 'hard-nosed facts'.

We touch on a very delicate question here, one that bears not only on the visionary world of the Celtic tradition but primarily on the visionary world of Christian revelation. There are those who see the events recorded in the New Testament, such as the Virgin Birth, the story of the multiplication of the loaves and fishes, the Resurrection and the Ascension, as rich and valuable symbols or myths which are not to be seen as factual or historical in the scientific sense. On the other hand, there are those who bring the light of factuality to bear on these events and, with a certain stubbornness, hold that this kind of question can be dealt with by putting faith first, and the greatness of the Power of God. Is it not possible that these events may indeed be factual and historical, provided we open the doors of perception just a little, and not close these doors firmly with a certain kind of question and questioning. It might seem a sensible question to ask whether Mary did or did not become a mother in the usual way, yet this kind of question rules out every possible category of birth except the physical and the physical-corruptible at that, although we are talking of the conception of a Being who will never see corruption. So, too, if I ask whether the physical body of Jesus was resuscitated at the Resurrection I am asking a question within the narrowest limits of the doors of perception, a question that does not really open to the mystery of the Word made Flesh. The kind of question that we *can* ask will have to do with the imaginal context of these events, that is to say, questions concerning the kind of reality that is being opened up to us so as to put our everyday perceptions in question. God cannot be born of Mary unless we allow our perceived images of conception and birth to be extended. A man cannot rise from the dead unless our images of man and of death are extended.

What I am saying is that a certain kind of imagination is necessary if we are to open to the Celtic vision of nature, and that this imagination is also necessary to open to the world of the New Testament. It is an intimational rather than a scientific world, but nevertheless a *real* world, full of the one great Presence and showing itself in mysterious presences that are, as it were, the messengers of the Presence. These presences became intellectualised and rationalised in the meeting of the Christian message of salvation with Greek wisdom, but they did not disappear but rather shone with a special light. So too in the meeting of that same Christian message with Roman order and hierarchy. Here the presences found a human and temporal reflection and radiance in a hierarchical church and in a scholastic theology. In the Eastern Church these presences found their home in the great liturgies in which heaven and earth met and mingled in clouds of glory. To the Celtic tradition it was left to relate these presences to the King of Creation, Lord of the Elements, in that same Lord's elemental presence on earth and sea and sky, in mountain and valley, lake and river. All the figures of ancient imagination prepare and prefigure the coming of the one that Blake, near to this tradition, called 'Jesus the Imagination', Jesus shining forth in his risen glory in the Easter sun as it danced in the sky for those who awaited it on their own mountain.

III

It was these elemental presences that came up from the depths of memory, the Place of Hope according to John of Fontiveros, to comfort my father's spirit when he lay dying in the shiny brightness of a modern hospital. The memory of a day's fishing along a mountain stream, with rocks and heather all around, and the living brightness of the flowing water, was all he could talk of, somewhat to my distress then, over forty years ago, but now to my comfort in my own old age. That same nature from which he came, and with which he had lived all his life, was taking him back to that Presence beyond all presences to which we must all return. Here again, imagination lights the way and finds a pathway through the mothering presences to the ultimate Presence.

In all this nature does not speak but preserves an eternal silence behind all its murmurs. Yet, for the folk of the mountains, as for the folk of the valleys and the plains, Nature had its own voice. Once, in a playful mood, the sage I have already invoked tried to give human utterance to the voice of nature. We read in Chapter 4 of the eighth treatise of the Third Ennead of Plotinus: 'Nature, asked why it brings forth its works, might answer if it cared to listen and to speak: It would have been more becoming to put no question but to learn in silence just as I myself am silent and make no habit of talking. And what is your lesson? This: that whatsoever comes into being is my vision, seen in my silence, the vision that belongs to my character who sprung from vision, am vision-loving and create vision by the vision-loving faculty within me. I gaze, and the figures of the material world take being as if they fell from my contemplation.'[13]

All this is light and vision, and it speaks of the goodness of creation in terms of a strong philosophical imagination that is echoed by the religious folk imagination of the Celtic tradition. Yet this is but one of the two moods of this imagination. There is another mood, one in which nature brings death and sorrow, and echoes in its darker moods the griefs and derelictions of the human heart. The history of the Celtic peoples is a litany of natural and military calamities leading to almost total humiliation and marginalisation. Lamentation has a central part in Celtic poetry and music, and the *Ban Caointe*, the Wailing Woman, had an honoured place in every community. She gave voice to the grief of a people for whom death was very much part of life, and for whom hunger and homelessness were

---

[13]McKenna translation. See also *The Essential Plotinus* by Elmer O'Brien. O'Brien calls this passage a bad joke that must be taken very seriously.

always near. The mountain behind the mountain was all the more a place of dreams because the mountain itself was often a place of hardship and meagre fruitfulness. We shall return to this theme in our final chapter.

Yet what is remarkable about this tradition is that it received, and still receives, the Christian story and the message of salvation, not as a release and liberation from calamity, but rather as providing meaning and significance. So it was with the Son of Mary, the Son of God, and should *we* seek anything different or humanly more comfortable? Not that there was that indelible sense of sinfulness and divine wrath that one finds in some other Christian traditions, but rather a sense that God and man are somehow in all this together, and that the Divine Man has suffered in his innocence more than we in our obvious imperfection could ever suffer.

In all this, Nature is seen as good and holy, invaded and menaced by fallen spirits, but so good in itself that we can invoke the elements themselves as a protection, as in the Breastplate of St. Patrick. Thus it is that Nature itself is in the Celtic imagination always a friend to humankind, always in touch with the ancient world of the Old and New Testaments. No wonder that its portals open towards a region of light and hope in life and in death.

4

THE PILGRIMAGE TO 'THE CITY'

I

The City which lies in the shadow of the Breasts of Dana was never a city in the usual sense of the word. The word 'City' translated the immemorial word *Cathair*, which means primarily a fortress or fortified place. It was this word I was hearing when, as a small boy, I saw the women crossing the hill at Beltane, though by then the *Cathair* was not even a fortified place. Today it is no more than a field, a small stream and well, and a heap of stones; indeed, I had some trouble in locating it when I made my own pilgrimage there some years ago. But there, at the foot of the mountain, the City has its own atmosphere and a kind of timelessness in which Anu and Muire are one, as with a kind of shock one recalls that Anna or Ann is honoured all over the Christian world as the Mother of Mary conceived without sin. In its elemental wild simplicity this place might be Lourdes or Fatima or Knock or Medjugorje. By contrast with all these places the City that is neither city nor *Cathair* has maintained its original elemental wildness and simplicity. Yes, there is still the annual pilgrimage, never quite defunct and revived some years ago, yet as I stood there alone I could only rejoice that I could breathe in something of that solitude that Mary of Nazareth knew as she carried her child within her to the hill country of Judea, that solitude which is the gateway to the eternal companionship of the angels and saints, and of Mary's Son.[14]

But of course the annual pilgrimage keeps alive the tradition of the City, and we can only be grateful that it was revived in 1925. And here, I think, it is right to salute a remarkable man, Fr. William Ferris, later Parish Priest of Glenflesk, and later still of Ballylongford, but then, in 1925, a curate at Rathmore, and no doubt the main agent in the revival of the pilgrimage. At any rate, according to Daniel Cronin's account, Fr. Ferris preached the sermon on that occasion and made a clear link between the ancient Goddess of the Mountain and the Virgin Mary. 'It is most fitting' said Fr. Ferris, 'that the festival is held on the first day of Our Lady's month, for the Mother of God, in the person of Dana, has been worshipped here for hundreds of generations.'

These are strong words, and quite unwittingly, they provide a clue to the reason why Mary, the Mother of God, did not appear in Irish devotion until the eighth century. For, though the word 'worship' may be applied correctly to the pre-Christian cult of Dana, it cannot be correctly applied to the Christian and Catholic cult of Mary. If Mary had been given her rightful place from the beginning, her place as defined by the Council of Ephesus in the fifth century, then she would

---

[14] All that I know about the City, *Cathair Crobh Dearg* as it is called, comes to me from two pieces of writing by Daniel Cronin, the one published in the *New Review* and entitled 'Kerry, Home of the Gods and of God,' and another, in typescript, called 'Danaan History,' and based on the researches of an Irish-American named O'Kief, as well as on Dan's own considerable knowledge of local legends and traditions. Apart from Dan Cronin's articles, I consulted that outstanding book on the ancient Irish traditions, *The Feast of Lughnasa* by Marie MacNeill. This book put everything in a wider context, but did not really add anything new to what I had learned from Daniel Cronin. This chapter is the text of a talk given in Dingle, Co. Kerry, in 1989.

indeed in people's imagination assume the status of a goddess to be worshipped. This would be the wrong kind of assumption and the wrong understanding of Mary. Mary did not come as a goddess far above human pains and griefs and the pathos and terror of our little existence. No, she came as one of ourselves, and she is, and always will be, one of ourselves. This is what mainly I want to talk about, and in order to do so I want to leave my mountain behind for a while and travel across the Irish Sea, first to the Highlands and Islands of Scotland, and then to another kind of city than the City of *Crobh Dearg*, the city of London. Two men will lead me on in my pilgrimage of understanding Mary of Ireland, the one a very Scottish Scotsman, Alexander Carmichael, and the other a very English Englishman, G. K. Chesterton.

II

Alexander Carmichael fell in love with the marginalised Gaelic culture of those islands that lie along the western seaboard of Scotland and have, even to this day, held on to their native culture and language: that Scottish Gaelic that is just as close to the Irish of Donegal as this latter is close to the Irish of Munster. This language and this culture, though still extant, has sadly diminished in our century, but Carmichael came just in time to salvage enough of it to fill (in original and translation) five large volumes published between 1900 and 1954 (see note 8 above). The contents of these volumes, hymns and prayers dating for the most part to the sixteenth century, are unique in Christendom in the beauty of the language, in the freshness of the imagery, and the depth and immediacy of the piety expressed in a kind of domestic liturgy centred around the homestead and the little world of island crofting communities.

In these hymns, prayer and blessings Mary is present as part of a spiritual atmosphere that pervades all the experiences, concerns and vicissitudes of life. There is no question of any special apparitions of Mary, though she is specially remembered at certain times, and specially invoked at times of crisis. She had her place of unique honour among the heavenly presences: the 'Three', Christ (frequently referred to simply as the 'Son of Mary'), the Angels in their hierarchies, the sainted dead, who are very much alive. The people who made these poems and prayers were poor folk who knew adversity, injustice, and all the shadows and terrors of life, but they had a constant sense of the presence of the hidden world and the protection of those gentle and powerful beings that crowded round the hearth and filled every nook and cranny of space and time. In this atmosphere Mary is the 'banatee', the woman of the house, and every woman of the house stays close to Mary.

These voices from the past are not at all alien voices to us here among the mountains of Kerry. They are the voices of our common heritage, and the woman they tell us of is the woman we know. In other places in the wide Christian world Mary has the status of a queen, with some of the features of a goddess. Mary of Ireland, whose name appears in the everyday greeting *'Dia is Muire Dhuit'*, is no far-off goddess or queen, but fitting rather the title of *'banatee'*, or even the title of *cailin amsire* the kind of *cailin aimsire,* who left our shores to enter service in the New World, and brought along with them the jewel of true devotion hammered out in the forge of daily toil and constancy.

This brings me to G. K. Chesterton, the London journalist,one of the greatest writers of our time, who found his spiritual home first in Christianity, then in the Catholic form of Christianity, and finally in that Catholic understanding of Mary that he found in Ireland. Some time before he died he decided to donate an ikon of Mary to his local church at Beaconsfield, near London, and went to a large Catholic repository to find the ikon or statue that represented most faithfully his inner vision of Mary. None of them satisfied him, and finally the manager of the store led him to a room behind the shop containing statues that had been put away as unsuitable or unfashionable. There he came on a statue of Mary of Ireland as a barefoot colleen carrying a child wrapped in a rough shawl, and he said: 'This is it'. Chesterton had recalled a story he had heard in Ireland according to which somebody at the time of the Great Famine met a barefoot girl walking across a wild mountain in wild weather carrying a child, and when the man asked her who she was replied: 'I am Mary and this is the Boy you will all be wanting at the end'. It is perhaps nothing much as a story, but it sparked off in Chesterton the vision he needed and the comfort he needed. Neither Mary of Walsingham in her dignity nor Mary of the great Italian painters in her glory, met the need he felt for the Mother of God who was truly one of ourselves and whose son was truly God-with-us, walking the common earth in common daylight, a mother and child, poor and clear and simple, walking a wind-swept mountain pathway. In her bare feet and rough shawl she could have passed without comment among the women that I saw more than sixty years ago passing across the Breasts of Dana on their way to the City on the first of May.[15]

III

Mary of Ireland, in all her simplicity, freshness, vulnerability and strength, must surely bear a very close resemblance to the woman that shines briefly and yet powerfully across the narrative of the Gospels. She is not just a symbol or archetype, as described by Carl Jung and certain Christian symbolists such as Mary Warnock. She is a historical person, not a 'mythical' being such as Dana or Banba or the Queen of the

---

[15] See O'Donoghue, 'Chesterton in Ireland: a mystical pilgrimage'. *The Chesterton Review*, November 1984 (Vol. X, no. 4) pp. 376-400.

Shee. She comes to us along the road of history, a road continuous with our everyday experience. Yet we reach Mary also along the road of imagination, not the road of fanciful or fictional imagination, but the road of imagination as a deepening of perception, the road of a visionary imagination that leads deep into the heart as love, and the mind as an inner vision of truth, beauty and goodness. We are here in the world of spiritual vision, of that pure light beyond all images and all imagination, a light that nevertheless shines into the depths of our powers of perception.

For according to ancient writers such as Ambrose and Augustine in the fifth century, and Thomas and Bonaventure in the thirteenth, we have within us five internal or spiritual senses revealing inner worlds to be seen and heard, even to be touched and tasted at times, and felt as fragrance filling the depths of the soul, so that it seems, to use the words of John of the Cross, 'all the perfumes of the whole world were shaken together'. It is here that Mary meets us if we are pure enough to meet her. Perhaps we may meet her for a moment in times of deep distress. Children may meet her in a kind of sharing of this inner world of perception , and she comes clothed in the garments of their imagination bearing messages and secrets.[16]

There can be real contact here with Mary and the angels, and even physical miracles of compassion and healing may be wrought, as happened and still happens outstandingly at Lourdes. Here in Ireland, people's inner perception of Mary showed itself in the phenomenon of the moving statues. No doubt some of this was mere fancy, but I feel that essentially there was question rather of spiritual perception finding a foothold as it were, in the statues or ikons. Indeed, for those

---

[16]See Père Poulain, *The Graces of Interior Prayer*. London, Kegan Paul, 1928. Also 'The Ignatian Prayer of the Senses' by Philip Endean, *Heythrop Journal*, XXI, 1990, pp. 391-418.

who truly understand sacred ikons, these ikons are always in movement. That is the very nature of an ikon, that it should communicate its meaning to our spiritual senses as they become attuned to the spiritual ambience that the ikon represents.[17]

We are here in the world of piety, of Marian piety as expressed by the recitation of the Rosary, *An Coróinn Mhuire*, the Crown of Mary, in her meditation and mediation of the saving and transforming work of her Son, who crowns her as his consort, as Queen of Heaven. However, this kind of piety can become self-enclosed unless it expresses itself in practical charity and compassion. It can also become narrow and self-righteous unless it connects with *wisdom* and the quest for understanding, including the understanding of other Christian faiths and other religious traditions. This means reaching out in respect and understanding to that pre-Christian perception of the gods and goddesses which is part of the road which our people have travelled. Those women and those men who crossed the mountain to the ancient *cathair* are our kin, and they are still with us.

But Mary of Ireland does not enclose us in our Irishness or in our history. She walks the hills of Antrim where she is little known or seemingly rejected as well as the hills of Kerry. She walks the streets of London as the hidden companion of people's loneliness and longing. She stands for the true awakening of the feminine in the Christian and non-Christian world. We who know her want to share her and her presence perceived and hidden in our lives, now and especially at the hour of our death.

---

[17]One gets this impression especially in the Ikon Chapel in Glenstal Benedictine Abbey at Murroe, Co. Limerick, Ireland.

5

THE PRESENCE OF GOD IN THE *CARMINA GADELICA*

I

Two great men who flourished around the turn of the 19th–20th centuries have managed to preserve for us, and for the future, something of the old Celtic culture of Ireland and Scotland: one is Douglas Hyde, the Anglican scholar who became, in his later years, President of the Catholic Irish Republic, and who spent most of his life collecting, and putting before the public, what he could discover of the ancient Irish lore still surviving in the West of Ireland. Two collections are specially memorable: *Dánta Grá Cúige Connacht* (Love Songs of Connaught) and *Dánta Diaga Cúige Connacht* (Religious Songs of Connaught), and this latter especially could be drawn on to illustrate our theme of the presence of God in the Celtic tradition. But the work of the other scholar is even more relevant to our theme, and so I shall simply salute Douglas Hyde and his folk of the Irish Western World and pass on to draw on the riches collected by Alexander Carmichael (1832–1912) in the Highlands and Western Islands of Scotland.[18]

The richness and depth, the ever-present reality of the Presence of God in the very simple homes of the people of the Highlands and Islands at the end of the last century is most vividly conveyed by the prayers connected with the smooring

---

[18]See note 8 above.

of the fire at night and the kindling of the same fire in the morning. When I was a boy this was still happening in my own home under the Breasts of Dana in the south of Ireland. We had the same kind of peat fire as Carmichael's crofters and cotters, and nightly the fire was smoored, or smothered, by putting a few small shovelfuls of the brown-yellow sifted ashes on the remaining coals, which, somewhat diminished but still alive and glowing, could be used to build a new fire in the morning. Thus the fire on the hearth was never really extinguished.

This recovery and rebuilding of the fire in the early morning has, in my memory, something of magical renewal about it, and ritually marked the beginning of a new day. Nowadays one goes into the kitchen or sitting-room and turns on the light and the fire. Some people still use solid fuel, with as a rule much rattle and clatter that does little or nothing to welcome a new day, except that at some point a natural naked flame emerges and one is for a moment in touch with an archetypal image of life and renewal. One way or another the situation does not call forth the consciousness and the voices and gestures of ritual.

Let us, however, use the blessed and indestructible power of imagination and enter into the consciousness and expression of a woman or man from Carmichael's world as a new fire is built and a new day welcomed. Carmichael's English translation, variously taken over by others, is sufficiently clear and lively, though it does not, nor could it, convey much of the felicitous verbal echoes and interweaving of sound and sense of the Gaelic original.[19] I shall try to indicate some of these as we go along, but all the time I want you to hold the image of a woman or man bending over the fireplace in a roughly-built thatched cottage of a morning at first light in uncertain Highland weather.

---

[19] See *The Sun Dances*, p. 3 and, especially, the Gaelic original in *Carmina Gadelica* Vol. I, p. 230.

This is the prayer that she or he recites bending over the kindling: The first stanza names the work of the kindling, and, as it were, opens the door to the angelic presences: *Aingle naofa neiv*, literally 'the holy angels of heaven'. The angels fill the little cottage, and at their centre is the Holy Son of God: *naov mach Dé*. This first stanza moves on to the form of a protection prayer, reminding us that the theme of protection is central to Celtic prayer wherever we find it. Here the word *Tarmad*, 'shield' or 'shielding', binds together this first stanza of the prayer, and serves, as it were, to cleanse and purify the whole ambience of the day's beginning, placing it in the Holy Presence of God. Quite often Celtic protection prayer names the enemies of the human soul, especially Satan and his minions, thus following the last two petitions of the Lord's Prayer. Here, however, the enemies against which protection is invoked are the dark thoughts of the human heart: malice, jealousy, envy and the rest. Fear is also named, and this is seen as the presence of the enemy, but the general force of the prayer as protective looks to the human heart and will.

The second stanza introduces a depth and subtlety that must not be missed if the prayer is to be understood. It has to do with 'the heart within' *(mo chree steach)* and the kindling within the heart of a fire that mirrors and transcends the external fire on the hearth:

God kindle Thou in my heart within
A fire of love to my neighbour.

Aingeal ghrá, literally, an angel or brightness of love: the angels of the first stanza are at once real presences and moral presences. This fire or brightness of love shines out to all: 'to my foe, to my friend, to my kindred all'. This is traditional Christian charity in all its nobility of living, but the prayer goes even further, and strikes a note that is perhaps unique to Celtic Christianity. For the fire and brightness of love goes out to the whole of nature 'from the lowliest thing that lives/to the Name that is highest of all'.

This love, for all that lives in a total unity of life, is all too rare in Western civilisation and Western Christianity, though perhaps it has a place in certain forms of Neo-Platonism where, as in Plotinus, the theme of a world-soul is prominent, and there may even be a connexion between the ancient Celts and the ancient Greeks. Indeed, this simple prayer, uttered by a crofter in the dusk of a highland morning, affirms clearly and concisely the whole philosophy of that Green Revolution which has been painfully forced upon us as we awaken to the terrible things we have done to the living earth and all that lives around us and gives us life.

There are many such prayers of kindling, or 'making of the fire', in the Carmichael collection, and they all show the same quality of close relationship to the heavenly presences and to the world of nature. But these were not always seen as the first prayers of the day, for there were 'rising' or 'morning' prayers as well, of which the second prayer in 'The Sun Dances' is typical, with its simple and powerful images of protection and purification:

> Even as I clothe my body with wool
> Cover Thou my soul with the shadow of Thy wing.

There is here a very perfect correspondence and unity of body and spirit, affirming not dualism but integration. This is strengthened by another image in which external nature is made to mirror the ongoing process of spiritual purification that is at the heart of all prayer.

> And as the mist scatters on the crest of the hills
> May each ill haze clear from my soul, O God.
>
> ('S mar a sgaoileas an céo air ceann nam beanniu
> Gur sgaoilea gach sgeohack var manam a Dhé)

So it is that each act of the daily round is taken into a kind of domestic liturgy linking heaven and earth, *There* and *Here*.

II

The morning prayers of rising and kindling are complemented and completed, in Carmichael's collection, by the night prayers of smooring or smothering the fire and lying down to sleep. They have the same character of personal and household concreteness and 'situatedness' that yet opens outwards and upwards to the whole of nature and to the angelic and divine regions. The little poem/prayer named 'Repose' by Carmichael is at once perfect and typical:

> Thou being of marvels
> Shield me this night
> Thou being of Statutes
>   and of stars.
>
> (A Hee nan reackt
> Agus nan Roille.)[20]

Here the Supreme Being is at once a being of marvels to be admired and a being of statutes to be obeyed. 'Two things', says the great philosopher Immanuel Kant, 'fill the mind with wonder and awe: the starry sky above and the moral law within'. The golden thread of wisdom shines so clearly here, connecting the crofter and the philosopher, that one is left wondering whether some ancient school of philosophy, lost in the mists of time, lies behind both the crofter's prayer and Kant's great vision that may not be unconnected with his Scottish ancestry.

[20] The invocation of the Source of Deity as *Hee* is connected with *Tay* or *Tee*, being indeed *tee* aspirated or breathed on: a *Hee*. *Tee* is a very personal invocation, and the aspiration gives it (as with all vocatives) a kind of closeness of I and Thou that in general gives Gaelic a special kind of intimacy as a language of prayer.

The prayer descends from the universal to the personal — calling on the 'being of statutes and of stars' to keep, shield, encompass the sleeper this night and every night 'both soul and body'. In the Celtic tradition this dualism of soul and body is common, but it is clearly a dualism of aspect rather than a dualism of separation. This point will come up again. Here it is clear that the duality of the soul and body connects with two other dualities, both of which are complementary:

> Compass me aright
> Between earth and sky
> Between the mystery of Thy laws
> And my eye of blindness.
>
> *(Eadar rún do reachd*
> *Acus dearc mo dhoille)*

In these two lines a whole theology shows itself, comes out of concealment. God, the Source, the supreme personality, is close to humanity, and this prayer asks for an even greater and deeper closeness. But this closeness pierces and purifies; it searches out all the hidden veins of selfishness and self-conceit; it is, in the image of St. John of the Cross, a strong lye or acid that penetrates the very substance of the soul, that challenges in the name of ultimate goodness my own clouded and self-excusing vision of myself. Each of us, says Kathleen Raine, is our own blind-spot. We all know people who are full of talk about God and spirituality, and who are only concerned with their own ambitions and plans. One of the central truths of the New Testament is that it was the godly people, so-called and self-proclaimed, who killed the Son of God. This is an archetypal human situation which can be met only by this kind of prayer by which the eye of the heart opens beyond its own conceits to the humble acceptance of a higher light and a higher wisdom.

So it is that, in the final stanza of this precious and ancient morning prayer, a clear distinction is expressed between what is seen and understood and what lies beyond vision and understanding. The Divine Presence is invoked to encompass the one and the other.

> Both that which mine eye sees
> And what it sees not;
> Both that which is clear
> And is not clear to my devotion.
>
> (*Eadar na caí*
> *Agus nach lí mo shúil*
> *Eadar nas léir*
> *Agus nach léir dha m'rún.*)

The Presence of God is at once light and darkness, at once clarity and mystery.

III

The little poem or invocation that I want to look at now is to be found in Vol. III, p. 307, of the *Carmina Gadelica* of Alexander Carmichael and on p. 58 of *The Sun Dances*. Carmichael took it down from two old men, one in Mingulay, Barra, and one, who was 99 years of age, in the southern end of South Uist. As Carmichael translated it the invocation runs as follows:

> The eye of the great God
> The eye of the God of Glory
> The eye of the King of Hosts
> The eye of the King of the Living,
>
>> Pouring upon us
>> At each time and season
>> Pouring upon us
>> Gently and generously.

Glory to Thee
Thou glorious sun
Glory to thee thou sun
Face of the God of life.

The translation is a fairly literal one, though the somewhat awkward repetition of 'glory' in lines 10 and 11 is avoided in the Gaelic. What is important, here as elsewhere, is that Carmichael does not in any way try to soften the force of the direct invocation of the sun nor take its glory as a metaphor for the glory of God, though the sense of metaphor is not missing or excluded. What is true is that the literal is not absorbed by the metaphorical. If the supernatural, the divine transcendant, is not reduced to the natural in this ancient way of looking at physical nature, neither is the natural absorbed or taken up into the supernatural, so much so that at best the natural world is merely the theatre of God's glory, shown forth in the mystery of redemption, and has no glory of its own in its original creation. In this song the bright glory of the sun does not disappear into heavenly glory but continues to reflect the heavenly glory, the face of the God of Life. God, the all-holy source and creator, is *present* within the sun, appears through the sun, clothes itself with the sun as a kind of garment — not however in a material spatial sense as belonging to that which passes away and is subject to corruption, but in a spiritual sense, the sense in which St. Paul speaks of the spiritual body, *soma pneumatikon*, of the world of the Resurrection (I Cor.15).

Here we are touching on a special vision of Creation, known to the ancient Celts as it was known to St. Paul and the ancient schools of Israel and Greece, something that has faded and disappeared over the centuries of scientific and technological progress. It can be argued quite reasonably that in the Divine Dispensation the potentialities and hidden energies of the material world had to be grasped and employed by man's skill and creative energies, and that in a sense the wonders of technology are among the great works of God by way of man and the latent powers of Creation. St. Teresa, in her homely way, tells us that God moves among the pots and pans; it can be said that God moves among the microscopes and telescopes.

Those old people who gave this invocation of the sun to Alexander Carmichael, as well as the old woman who told him of the sun dancing at Easter, were no light-headed enthusiasts, but had rather gained a deep mystical sense of the Great Presence by way of a long life of hardship and reflection by which this inner vision gradually awakened. What is most remarkable about Carmichael is that these people felt they could share their vision with him and find understanding. There is a moving story told by Carmichael himself. It tells of an old man from one of the far islands who shared a 'singularly beautiful going to sleep prayer' with him and was very happy to do so, until later on in his bed that night it came to him that Carmichael would share his prayer with others. The story goes on: 'Early next morning this reciter travelled twenty-six miles (by foot) to extract a pledge that his 'little prayer' should never be allowed to appear in print 'for he did not like cold eyes to read it in a book'. His request was granted, and his little prayer has not come down to us. He had told us, with devastating simplicity, that we are not worthy of it: we do not have the right warmth in the heart to hear it with our ears. It is worth noting that, for this old man, scholarship and academic competence were worse than useless: only the heart could 'hear' his 'singularly beautiful going to bed prayer'.

IV

At the other end of the scale from the invocation of the sun is the much longer poem called 'The Hatching Blessing', which has to do with the simple work of putting eggs under a hen for hatching. Like all work in this tradition and ambience, this work of putting the hen to hatching was seen in terms of a ritual which linked it up with the world around, and also with the heavenly bodies and with the heavenly presences.

> I will rise early on the morning of Monday
> I will sing my rune and my rhyme.
> I will go sunwise with my cob
> To the nest of my hen with sure intent.
> I will place my left hand to my breast
> My right hand to my heart
> I will seek the loving wisdom of Him (lit. of the Being)
> Abundant in grace, in broods and in flocks.

It is important to look closely at the gestures of this work-hymn. The woman — for it is and must be a woman who is involved — goes sunwise, *deiseal* (literally, 'by the right') with her little basket as she sets out to put the eggs to hatch, for thus she will have the energy of the all-nurturing sun going along with her as she goes towards the nesting-place of her hen who is, one assumes, a 'clocking' hen ready to hatch. In the order of nature the hatching hen completes her motherhood and by her 'clocking' makes it clear that she is ready for this. Commenting on the text where Jesus, in his most original simile, compares his love for humankind to that of a hen gathering her chicks under her wing, one of the fathers of the Church asks why this image is used, and he answers that the reason is that only the hen among animals and birds advertises its motherhood, so much so that even when no chicks are about you can see that the hen is a mothering hen. In hatching out her chicks the hen completes her motherhood, and so the woman who tends her points to her own motherhood, actual or potential, by placing her hands in a certain position before she begins, and making by way of her own body a connexion with the ultimate generative power of the all-wise Creator. (Alexander Carmichael, though he was deeply immersed in the Celtic world, was, after all, a Victorian translating for Victorians, so that here he misses the sharpness of the Gaelic original.)

In this way the woman's nurturing power enters into the work of hatching out the chicks, and by her prayer and attitude she makes the whole work a religious work held within the sacredness of Creation. This is a deep and delicate sense in which there is seen to be a kind of shadow of destructiveness menacing all nature and the uses of nature, and in which the close priestly presence of men and women is necessary by way of prayer and blessing. Nature itself is good in all its levels — the Augustinian and Lutheran doctrine of a total Fall is quite alien to this tradition — but Satan and his minions are always a menacing presence, and always the prayers of protection and consecration are necessary. There are also protective rituals which may appear meaningless and superstitious, and which may get detached from their original sacred connexion, but which in themselves, and in their original intention, are simply ways of affirming and calling forth the Divine Presence. In the hatching prayer and liturgy a little soot is put on the eggs as a kind of protective blessing which links the process with the family hearth and the fire constantly renewed.

V

The people of the *Carmina Gadelica* had a blessing for every work done on their little farms: weaving, milking the cows, shearing the lambs, sowing the seed, and so on. In each case the worker, man or woman, was seen to have a priestly role linking the divine with the human world, and bringing men and women into the processes of nature, usually in a delicately feminine or masculine way. Thus, in the sowing of the seed, the work was connected with a man's body and with the elements of wind and sun and soil as he strode along scattering the seed-corn or dropping the seed-potatoes prepared by the women for sowing.

The people of the *Carmina Gadelica* were deeply conscious of rhythms — the rhythms of human life and the body's ages and changes, the rhythms of the seasons, of work such as weaving and milking, of reaping with hook or scythe (though this latter was scarcely there in our grandfathers' times), of threshing the corn, of men rowing together, of women waulking together. All these rhythms, and many others, were vocalised in song and what was called *port-béul* or voice-music. Indeed, if one listens to the changes and cadences of Gaelic speech, one is drawn into the world of these rhythms, and this is the basis of what is called 'the Irish brogue'. Transformed into English in its Anglo-Irish or Lallans forms it has created the language of Synge, Yeats, Burns and MacDiarmuid, for those who have an ear for it a language variously full of enchantment and colour.

Song and music has been at or close to the centre of Gaelic life all through the ages, though there have been very dark times when these voices were muted and nobody had the heart to dance; yet in time the deep griefs and calamities of the people found their voice in the lament or *caoine*, by which the voice of pathos took on the force and beauty of that eternal pathos which is the basis of so much of the world's greatest poetry, from Homer right down to Yeats, Eliot, Hopkins, Sorley MacLean, and Seán O'Riordán. Nor has the presence of the *caoine*, or even in certain circumstances its predominance, obliterated the more joyful modes, nor that sense of fun that never forsook the people of the Highland clearances and the Great Irish Famine. The 18th and 19th were terrible centuries for the Celtic people of Ireland and Scotland, and, in different ways, for the whole marginalised Celtic world. It is deeply significant that the two great preservers of the Celtic past that have been mentioned, Alexander Carmichael and Douglas Hyde, arose like morning stars at the threshold of the 20th century, for this century has been the time of the gradual reawakening of the ancient Celtic people and what has been called 'the Celtic Consciousness' or 'Celtic Continuum'. That same long sad saga of emigration to America and Canada, which was, it seemed, the final death of a great ancient civilisation, proved to be the beginning of a new dawn in a new setting for these people, which their children made their own and made great. It was, above all, the ancient music of pipe and harp that survived and took on new life and grace by way of the colours of memory and the self-discovery of a racial treasury of joy and beauty in song and dance.

The Celtic musical tradition is very varied in its modes and themes, but everywhere in the background there is the sound of the sea and the sound of the wind. The various traditions of set dancing and step dancing — rich in variety as each local community developed its own mode — have made the human body in its way a particularly graceful and subtle musical instrument expressing all human moods, and especially celebrating the rhythms of life in the mutual creativity of feminine and masculine that is most of all the basic rhythm of nature at all levels, nature vulnerable to degradation but profoundly open to resurrection and transformation.

6

THE HIDDEN PRESENCES

I

The people of the *Carmina Gadelica* lived in a world of many dimensions, some of them entirely hidden from our modern eyes. These dimensions opened up in many directions, opened into regions down in the depths but more especially upwards to 'The Sacred Three' and 'the Name that is Highest of all'. It is because of the hidden presence of these regions that an event or gesture or ritual or word occurring in the everyday world tended to gather around it a kind of cluster, or precipitate, of significances that could open to the dark as well as the light, and could thus sometimes appear as at once superstitious and dangerous.[21]

---

[21] Superstition can arise through fear or through malevolence. In both cases the user of the superstitious observance is really affirming the presence of an unseen world where things that seem insignificant or non-significant in the light of ordinary perception and belief in God acquire a significance that is threatening to human beings. In the depths of our beings, we all at times fear destruction and annihilation, and this can become a constant companion as we become old and feeble. Superstitious observances can be a way of dealing with that, a false way but not a wicked way. The true way of dealing with this fear and panic is to pray within the prayer world of Gethsemane and Calvary — 'Father if it be possible ...' 'My God, my God, why hast thou forsaken me?' Such prayer is also given voice in some of the psalms: 'Out of the depths have I cried to Thee, oh Lord' etc. These prayers come from deep within the human spirit, where the Holy Spirit meets the human spirit and teaches us how to find voice and speech. 'With inarticu-

It is not difficult to understand the desire of Catholic priests, and especially of the ministers of the Reformation, to clear all this away and present the plain Gospel in a plain setting untouched by imagination. What is not so easy to understand, as we read, for instance, what Carmichael describes in the General Introduction to his great work, is the extreme passion and self-satisfied zeal with which this cleansing of the temples was carried out, involving as it did the extirpation of so much innocent human gaiety and sharing. A kind of coldness and fear of life seemed to freeze the imagination and put a stop to all song and dance. This did not come from the frozen North and the Arctic seas but rather from the South and the soft

late groanings' (*Roman* 8). In these prayers we are opening up to the Presence of God by way of the Absence of God, and out of these dark prayers of the Absence of God there arise, sometimes when we least expect them, deep and precious touches of the Presence of God, because the darkness has cleansed and purified the soul. But those people who do not meet the challenge of the end of life can become weak and clinging, both in their dependence on others and in their relationship with God. The Celtic way lends itself to vain and superstitious observances at this point, but apart from this, the kind of old person who falls into a dependence syndrome will find other ways to express it. This kind of thing can be exasperating to others and can be despised by the young, who nevertheless, may well ask themselves how they will cope with illness and old age themselves.

Far different is that malevolent superstitious observance where rituals are undertaken in order to do harm to others. Of course, more than in anything else, this kind of evil returns to those who perpetrate it. The way for the intended victim is to ignore it entirely, or laugh at it, or invoke the Holy Presences against it. In the background of this malevolence and maleficence is a profound truth that the way we feel in our heart for others tends to externalise itself in a kind of dark and destructive energy field. We may feel this as a kind of heaviness or even a kind of needfulness that draws us in or sucks us in. Again, prayer and more prayer is the only answer in the long run to this kind of psychological attack and demand on us. But it is a problem which arises in one form or another in every life style and not just in the Celtic one alone.

climes of France and Italy, coming in the forms of Puritanism and Jansenism, shrouded in fear and all the terrors of hell and damnation.

All this added up to a false asceticism that affirmed death against life, sadness against joy, containedness against celebration, despair against hope. What the people of the *Carmina Gadelica* possessed already, and what shines forth clearly from the pages of Carmichael, is the asceticism of hard work, of a living discipline of prayer and practical charity, of a deep sense of, and deep involvement with, the presence of God as Creator and Incarnate in the 'Son of Mary'. Without this asceticism the way of life of the *Carmina* could not survive in its purity for more than a generation. That it managed to keep its bloom for several generations, and indeed several centuries, is a great wonder. That its memory has come down to us with such purity and beauty is no less a wonder, and also a challenge to those who realise its uniqueness and preciousness to kindle anew that fire that has lain so long in the ashes of its smooring.

II

It is against this background that we must try to understand the place of the angelic and other 'heavenly' presences in the Celtic tradition. The five senses present us with a constant ambience of sights and sounds and the rest. The angelic world opens up at the margins of this world where a certain kind of imagination reveals tentatively and faintly, never obviously, a world of light so delicate and tenuous that it is blown away by both dogmatism and scepticism. It is a perception that needs to work through prayer, and that needs to be protected by a tradition of belief that must not harden into dogmatism. The poets of nature, such as Wordsworth and Hopkins, have made living contact with this tradition. Wordsworth looks behind the phenomena or 'appearances' of nature, and discovers within himself 'a sense of something deeply interfused' which has its dwelling 'in the light of setting suns and the round ocean and the living air'. Hopkins finds ' the dearest freshness deepdown things', and makes the startling statement that when a human perceiver looks carefully and steadily at something in nature that thing looks back at him.[22] So, too, in our own day, T. S. Eliot finds in the squalor of an urban wilderness the presence of 'an infinitely gentle, infinitely suffering thing'.[23]

We are here in the company of the great poets who were 'different' from the ordinary folk around them, and seen as different or even odd or *very* odd. The people of the *Carmina Gadelica* were *all* poets in the sense that they all lived within a way of perceiving the world that opened up beyond the margins of the physically measurable and scientifically controllable. So when they spoke of angels they did not mean beings that could be seen or encountered in an everyday sense, measured and photographed and catalogued. On the other hand, they did not think of the spirit world as less real and less important than the ordinary measurable world with which the spirit world was interfused. Not *less* real but *more* real, then, as dwelling in the region of the timeless and incorruptible. So it is that when, in the *Blessing of the Kindling*, the kindler begins by saying: 'I will kindle my fire this morning/In the presence of the holy angels of heaven', he/she is affirming a real presence, a real 'coming into presence', a real coming into the company of presences: *an láhair* is a strong phrase affirming daylight and the openness of beings to each other. All philosophers in the Great Tradition see being, reality, not in terms of physical matter but rather in terms of presence, openness, and what is

---

[22] See Robert B. Martin's *Gerard Manley Hopkins*, Harper Collins, 1991, p. 203. Hopkins' words are: 'What you look hard at seems to look hard at you.' Here the word 'seems' expresses empathy rather than fancy.
[23] *Preludes* iv in *The Complete Poems and Plays of T. S. Eliot*. Faber and Faber, 1969, p. 22.

called 'intentionality', that is to say, that outreach by which I am most my own being in opening to the being of others. The presence of the holy angels of heaven is not a weak and pious wish but the affirmation of the presence of 'fire-making being' in its full ambience as immortal spirit. If somebody were to come into that little cottage at this time (or at any time) the visitor would be addressed by the kindler in the words *dia dhaoibh ar maidin*, that it, God be with ye in the morning. *Ye* not *You*, for the visitor's guardian angel is included in the greeting. This greeting remained among the folk of Kerry mountains even in my own time. It tells very simply of that common acceptance of the spiritual companions of men and women that was part of their own ancient culture.

There was a sense in which all mankind — certainly all the people of the *Carmina* and the Celtic world — was understood to have a special and powerful guardian angel named Michael, the same as appears as the leader of the Angels of God in chapter 12 of the Apocalypse. Michael, whose name denotes likeness with El or God, is seen as 'God's warrior man', leader of the whole host of Angels. He seems to have been given a human face and form, but was in no way a man born of woman as was 'the loveliest Son of Mary'. It is a delicate matter to distinguish the place of Michael in human and cosmic affairs in this tradition, but in this it simply reflects the original mystery of the Incarnation according to which Jesus Christ is almost always closely connected with the angels, right from his birth to his Ascension into the 'clouds of heaven'. What is clear all the way is that Jesus Christ belongs within the world of 'the Three' and that Michael and the angels are within the world of the divine and eternal but not within the world of 'the Three' or Trinity.

A song such as *Michael Militant* (S.D. p.107, C.G.III p. 145) sums up the various aspects of the Michael presence in the tradition, especially the function of guardianship of land and sea, and shielding against the foe, that is to say, Satan and his 'angels'. Humanity is seen as always attacked by or menaced by the Dark Powers, so that prayer-songs such as 'Michael Militant' served the very practical purpose of protection against these forces in life's journey:

> Be with us in the journey
> And in the gleam of the river

This last phrase is mysterious, and Carmichael does not attempt to explain it; it is somehow pictorially and imaginatively right, as is true of many strange turns of phrase in the *Carmina*. It is perhaps well that these lovely ancient songs and prayers should not yield all their mystery to our scientific probings, and that the people of the *Carmina* should hide from us some of their most secret and sacred feelings.

III

Now and then in the *Carmina Gadelica* we come across references to evil beings and forces contrary to human well-being. Only now and then, only here and there, but enough to let us see that these folk were deeply conscious of the Adversary, variously named, variously personalised. In the 'Consecration of the Seed' we find that the Carlin or Cailleach has to be faced and outfaced in the final stanza, and there is a sense in which almost all the prayers of the *Carmina* are protection prayers that call in the good and holy spirits and forces, and keep the evil spirits and forces at a safe distance. There is never question of destroying the evil entities, but rather of keeping them at bay, of being simply protected against them; in this the Celtic tradition is here and elsewhere totally in tune with the way of Christ in the New Testament. Whether we look at the *Breastplate of St. Patrick* in the eighth century or the *Carmina* in the nineteenth century, we meet with the constant vision of the world of man and nature as good, yet as constantly menaced by evil destructive forces that can only be repulsed and put back in their own place by prayer in union with Christ and the Heavenly Presences.

It would, however, be naive to rule out the possibility of connivance and collusion on the part of men and women with destructive forces, variously understood and invoked. In this tradition, as it came down to the present writer among the mountains of the south of Ireland, there was, and to some extent still is, darkness as well as light, including the use of various ancient rituals to bring bad luck on the neighbour seen as an enemy. Alexander Carmichael saw clearly what was reflected in his own sincere and utterly trustworthy Christian perception of the people of the Highlands and Islands of Scotland. The people he met were mostly old men and women, chastened, deepened and ennobled by lives of elemental human experience, for whom in most cases the world beyond was very near and very real. What of a more earthy nature remained in their memories from the innocent and perhaps not so innocent wildnesses of youth, or what of evil touched them or confronted them in later years: none of this finds its way into the *Carmina* any more than the normal upheavals of belief in normal adolescence. These reforming ministers that appear in rather dark colours in Carmichael's *Introduction* to the first volume of the *Carmina* can scarcely be cleared of a certain arrogance and obtuseness, yet we cannot be fair to them unless we see that there was at times a darker side to the world of the *Carmina*. It is only now we are beginning to see that, in destroying the evil, these men went a long way to destroying one of the greatest spiritual achievements of Christendom.

There is a further region in the Celtic consciousness of other worlds that is by no means central to the *Carmina Gadelica* but does appear from time to time, without comment, as something generally taken for granted. Sometimes the beings of this region — the region of the Shee or Fairies — are connected with evil forces, as in the lengthy and lightsome song *In Praise of Mary* (S.D. p. 93, C.G. III p. 127), in which we find:

> Save me from sky-hosts of evil
> And from fairy shafts. *(cuspoireann Síodh)*

But as a rule the *Shee* or *Leannawn Shee* were not so much evil as mischievous, capable of leading humans a merry dance if they were interfered with. Even in my own day I have known people to avoid building a house on a fairy rath or tumulus. These beings were closely connected with certain places or certain trees or shrubs, and had to be treated with respect, and sometimes even placated. Some of the poems of Yeats and George William Russell incorporate part of the folk-beliefs concerning the 'Hosts of the Air', the fairy-folk or *Leannawn Shee*, and those who are familiar with the system of Rudolf Steiner find in these works a whole cosmology of nature-spirits which belongs to the same world as the Celtic fairy-folk. As far as I know, the only general work of a scholarly nature devoted to the topic is *The Fairy-Folk in Celtic Countries* by W. Y. Evans-Wentz noted in our first chapter.

IV

In the Celtic tradition, as lived by the people of the Kerry Hills as well as the people of the *Carmina Gadelica*, death was intimately and positively part of life. Not for them the cold dictum of a modern philosopher that 'death is not an event in life'. Rather death and life were intimately mingled as basic colours of the one fabric that owed its unique and terrible beauty to that same intimate blending of colour and texture. '*Bás Sona*, happy death,' says Carmichael, 'is a phrase frequently heard among the people.' When these words are used they imply that the dying person has been 'confessed' and anointed, and that the death-hymn has been intoned over him. The old people wish, above all things on earth, that '*Bás Sona*' may be their own portion when the time comes for them to go' (Carmichael III, p.371). Death always involved companionship, the warm companionship of the living opening up to the mysterious companionship of those who had gone before, and who were seen as somehow present in the sacred space between earth and heaven.

There was a sense in which the women of the community took charge of death and dying, as they took charge of birth and the first baptising. Some women were particularly endowed with the art of 'keening the dead', and to hear their voices raised, and seeming to pierce the skies, was a tremendously impressive and deepening experience, especially for the young folk of the community. I recall the experience well, at my grandfather's waking, when I was a boy of twelve, though I did not realise then that I was destined to be a priest and a writer, and that this experience would all my life long enrich the very fabric of my attitudes to life and death, with an enormous power of lighting the darkness.

The final section of Volume III of the *Carmina Gadelica* is devoted to prayers connected with death and dying, and several of these are reproduced in the section 'Ages of Life' in *The Sun Dances*. They express a straightforward faith in God's power and presence, with clear and striking images, and a sense of the unity of nature and the supernatural.

> Thou great God of Salvation
> Pour Thy grace on my soul
> As the sun of the heights
> Pours its love on my body.

Here, as elsewhere in the Celtic Christian tradition, nature provides symbols and metaphors, yet the symbol, as of the sun and God's grace, is that bit more than a metaphor, and resists any kind of Cartesian dualism of Nature and Spirit. The warmth of the sun is a *loving* warmth, and all nature shows forth a mothering love, cherishing the soul in a way that is more than physical and yet has not lost the touch and tenderness of physical mothering. This appears with great poignancy in the hymn *I am going home with thee*, which on first reading might seem to be concerned with the death of a child.

I am going home with thee
Thou child of my love,
To thine eternal bed
To thy perpetual sleep.

But it was a common burial chant for those who died, old and young, men and women, and it expressed sorrow, peace and hope, but most of all it expressed homecoming to the Father's house. The tenderness of the words is the tenderness of a mother to her child, for we are all children in death and there is a sense in which only a mother can take us through that doorway, as only a mother can take us through the doorway of life. This archetypal motherhood was expressed by the whole community, and even by the all-mothering earth and the presences of nature. Carmichael's note on this burial chant is precious and memorable: 'This tune was played at funerals in Lewis, Harris and Skye down to Disruption times. I spoke to people who heard it played at a funeral at Aoidh, in Lewis. They said that the scene and the tune were singularly impressive — the moaning of the sea, the mourning of the women, and the mourning of the pipes over all, as the body was carried to its home of winter, to its home of autumn, of spring and summer; never could they forget the solemnity of the occasion, where all was so natural and so beautiful, and nature seemed to join in the feelings of humanity.' *(Carmina Gadelica III, p.379)*. What is essentially the same scene and the same 'feel' of death and human grief absorbed by the voices and holy presences of nature is present in that lovely song *Aignish on the machair* composed by Agnes Muir McKenzie, a contemporary of Alexander Carmichael and the people of the *Carmina*, and set to the music of a traditional Hebridean tune. It is to be found in Volume 3 of *Songs of the Hebrides* by Margery Kennedy Fraser and Kenneth McLeod.

There is a sense in which, for the people of the *Carmina*, the dead are always present in the elements and in the seasons and changes of nature, being as it were 'ministering angels', that is, human beings who are taken into the work of angels in the world 'beyond' that is within our everyday world. We meet them, not by 'seeing ghosts' but by sensing presences that belong with the angels and the timeless presences of heavenly glory and goodness, with Michael and Gabriel, with Bride and Mary, and with the Divine Son of Mary in whose light they dwell, 'the faithful departed'. It is towards this light that wandering spirits must be sent by prayer and love; it is towards the fulness of this light that the 'Holy Souls', the 'Good Dead', are travelling; and we, the living, are still their companions on the way, receiving as we give. But at this point we are perhaps becoming too narrowly theological. If we wish to stay with the people of the *Carmina* it is better to listen to the voices of wind and sea, and all they tell us than cannot be expressed in any formulation.

7

CELTIC CREATION SPIRITUALITY[24]

I

With a title such as 'Celtic Creation Spirituality' a speaker can go anywhere; each of these abstractions is like a boat in full sail on a wide sea with a strong following wind. Especially the word 'Celtic' can take us anywhere, on to Hy-Brasil, the Isle of the Blest, or onto the rocks of hard scholarship and the shattering of the fragile craft of imagination. That is one reason why I want to begin on the solid earth of lived personal experience, or, more imaginatively, within the glow of the peat fire flame, now long extinguished but central to my boyhood long ago in a thatched farmhouse on the Western Breast of Da Keek Anainn, the rounded breasts of Dana or Anna, goddess of the ancient time. The name remains, with many other names in that wild region in South Kerry, and these names tell the truth in their own way, telling of some event or of the presences of bird or animal or the *Leannawn Shee,* the invisible ones, that were companions of men and women in that place from the beginning.

But the point of entry into my theme, relating it to the earth and the fire constantly renewed on the hearth, is not a name but a phrase that was a prayer: *Buiochas le Dia*; Thanks be to God. 'Tis a fine day thanks be to God'. A solemn version of this

[24]From a talk given at the Catholic Theological Association Conference, 1990. See *The Month* (Nov. 1990) for the full text.

prayer was: 'Blessed be the Holy Will of God'. These words were spoken, I recall, by Mary Casey the moment she heard of the death of her two sons by drowning. John M. Synge captures some of the noble fatalism of this attitude in his 'Riders to the Sea', but, for all his genius and reverence, he remains outside this culture and its constant relation to the creative springs of life. For in this vision of life and death *all is gift*. In the beginning is the gift and the gift is with God and the Gift is God.

In what I see as his most readable book, a book written in his gentler later years, Martin Hedegger asks the question: *What is called thinking? (Was heisst Denken?),* and he transposes the question into another question: To what does thinking call us? He finds that thinking calls to thanking, linking *Denken* and *Danken*. For the woman whose heart was doubly pierced by the death of her sons thinking and thanking were one. So, too, Michael Sullivan, crippled by arthritis, who passed slowly and painfully along the *boreen* beside our house almost every day, thinking and thanking were not just closely connected but issued from the one breath: he would say as he stood by the gate 'Tis a fine day, thank God' or maybe 'Tis a wild day, thank God'. These are the voices of a people, it must be remembered, that had survived the dark centuries and such holocaust experiences as the Irish Famine, survived, like Job, still giving thanks to the Creator and the sources of life.

This is not the obsequious adoration of power, of a God who said *Let things be made* and they were made. This is not the kind of gift that is the object of this thanksgiving; this is not the kind of giving that is being received into the pierced heart of the woman or the tortured body of the man. The gift of Creation, however inarticulately, is a costly gift, as costly as the Passion and Death of Christ and the Seven Sorrows of Mary. The important point here, however, is that as one looks back along the road of this tradition there is no question of substituting a

Christo-centric for a theocentric theology; the Redemption does not swallow up nor push into the background the Creation and the created cosmos. Nature is not simply the theatre of God's glory or of Christ's redeeming presence. No, Christ is already there from the beginning, not simply as Saviour but as the centre of Creation in a Teilhardian sense as the going forth of the source, not simply as Word and *Fiat,* but as that outgoing *logos* through which all things are made. So, too, the Spirit is already there, for the spirits are already there, the Elohim of Genesis and the spiritual hosts of the Lord God of Hosts, the Lord of the Spirits of that mysterious Book or Books of Enoch that is so strangely present in the New Testament.

Creation was received thankfully by Mary Casey and by Michael Sullivan, as a gift shrouded in pain. The wild and terrible sea, the beautiful and cruel sea, had taken her two sons, helpless as newborn babes in their strong boast of manhood; the iron grasp of disease had held and crippled Michael's body, a man still young getting along painfully with two white-knuckled walking sticks cut from mountain ash by a local handyman. Creation came with pain, and the gift of Creation and the pain of the gift were received with equal thanksgiving. These people, like all the marginalised Celtic peoples, came out of great tribulation, hundreds of years of oppression culminating in the holocaust of the Great Famine, and so far were they from bitterness that every second word they spoke was a word of thanksgiving to the Creator of life and death, of joy and sorrow, of places and seasons, *Rí na Nûl,* the god of the elements, as I, the little boy whom they knew and whom they know in the 'land of the living', try to understand their way of being and their way of speaking. They were, of course, Irish Catholics. Catholics *du type irlandais,* a French intellectual of my generation would say, respectfully perhaps, but quite missing the meaning both of their way of being and their way of speaking. Perhaps John Betjeman was nearer the truth as he saw 'a stone-age people going between the fields to Mass'. He saw the enduring thing, but not the heart of that endurance, nor how the fields were part of it and the sky over the fields and the winds that could bring either blight or abundance. Perhaps Heinrich Böll in his *Irish Journal* comes nearest to this way of being human when he sees a lighthearted sense of survival at the heart of it all. Survival may be a kind of death, but to survive with humour and grace is quite another thing, and it was thus that Mary and Michael lived and spoke. The theologian must ask where it comes from and how it comes. And whether it can come again.

II

Mary's broken heart and Michael's broken body were both seen by their bearers as gift and a source of daily thanksgiving. I shall return to this and see it in the context of a certain vision and praxis of created nature in and around human kind as issuing in a daily liturgy of thanksgiving. But now I want to look more directly and generally at that attitude to created nature as gift and blessing that belonged to Celtic Christianity from the beginning, and which continues, however faintly, right up to our own day. In order to do this I want to take soundings within the deep waters of that common Christian heritage from which Mary and Michael emerge as witnesses. I shall take two such soundings, looking first at the eighth century *Lorica* or Breastplate which bears St. Patrick's name, and then at that Scottish collection of hymns and prayers from the sixteenth century and earlier collected by Alexander Carmichael under the general title of *Carmina Gadelica*.

The *Breastplate of St. Patrick* is a protection prayer, and as such fits in well with the Celtic vision of human life as menaced by evil forces and yet as in close everyday relationship and commerce with holy forces, with God as Trinity, with Christ as Saviour, with the great hosts of the angels and saints. *Loricae* or breastplates were common in ancient Christian Ireland. Many of them have come down to us, and some of them seem to indicate a continuity with pre-Christian prayers of the same kind. Human beings in all religious cultures have been conscious of the need for protection, not only in face of the vicissitudes and uncertainties of life but especially in relation to that other world of destructive demonic forces who, as in the case of Job, were allowed to sift and test human beings, sometimes in a most terrifying way: this is quite clearly and powerfully expressed in the last two petitions of the Lord's Prayer. It must be said, therefore, that the Breastplate prayer-tradition, though it echoes pre-Christian prayers of protection and deliverance, is by no means eccentric to the Christian doctrine and practice of prayer as we meet it in the New Testament.

This eighth-century prayer, the *Lorica Sanctii Patritii* provides a kind of window into a strange and familiar world, and I have tried elsewhere to look in a general way through this window.[25] Here I want to focus on the fourth stanza, in which the world of created nature is called in as a source of protection:

> For my shield this day I call:
> Heaven's might
> Sun's brightness
> Moon's whiteness.
> Fire's glory
> Lightning's swiftness
> Wind's wildness
> Ocean's depth
> Earth's solidity
> Rock's immobility.

[25] See *St Patrick's Breastplate* in J. P. Mackey (ed.) *An Introduction to Celtic Christianity*, T&T Clark: Edinburgh, 1987, pp. 45–63. See also p. 13 above.

Here the physical creation in all the elements appears as a shield and protection. There is question neither of a fallen, tainted world, nor yet of a world which is merely the theatre of God's glory. It is all good in itself and it provides comfort and protection against the dark powers that assail the body and the spirit (stanzas 6 and 7). It is noteworthy that each of the elements is seen in one of its qualities, qualities seen as expressing each some great natural force, as if each were somehow a messenger from the source, as that source variously manifests itself to human perception. These qualities are not seen as grasped or controlled by the mind but rather as calling the soul to wonder and adoration. God and Creation calls forth man's wonder, not man's questioning, for the questions would never be large enough nor sharp enough, and the wonder opens towards infinite horizons. The wonder and adoration is great enough to fill and heal the broken heart and the broken body. Creation is at once gift and mystery.

The invocation of nature in the *Breastplate* is immediately preceded by the invocation of the angels and the saints, the world of those presences that are everywhere in the Celtic Christian and pre-Christian tradition. This is the world of the angels in their shining order and also of the faithful departed, 'the good dead in the green hills', 'the holy and risen ones'.

> For my shield this day I call:
> strong power of the seraphim
> with angels obeying,
> and archangels attending,
> in the glorious company
> of the holy and risen ones,
> in the prayers of the fathers,
> in visions prophetic
> and commands apostolic,
> in the annals of witness,
> in Virginal innocence,
> in the deeds of steadfast men

This Irish world of nature and of the angels and saints is mirrored by the later Celtic world of the Scottish Highlands and Islands, the world of the *Carmina Gadelica* of Alexander Carmichael to which I now turn.

III

A whole book, indeed many books, could be written about the understanding of created nature that radiates through these prayers and poems in their elemental freshness, sharpness and simplicity.[26] They express a detailed domestic liturgy opening out to work in the fields and on the sea, and to the various concerns of a 'peasant' people. They are full of presence and full of presences, of a life lived in total relationship to a divine world. As in the *Breastplate of St. Patrick* there is in the *Carmina* a strong line of continuity between Christian and pre-Christian attitudes.

In order to look more concretely at all this I want to focus on a poem called 'The Consecration of the Seed', which is to be found on pages 242 and 243 of the first volume of the *Carmina* and on page 35 of *The Sun Dances*. It runs as follows in the Carmichael translation:

I will go out to sow the seed,
In name of Him who gave it growth;
I will place my front in the wind,
And throw a gracious handful on high.
Should a grain fall on a bare rock
It shall have no soil in which to grow;
As much as falls into the earth
The dew will make it to be full

Friday, day auspicious,
The dew will come down to welcome
Every seed that lay in sleep

[26]See note 8 above, Chapter 2.

Since the coming of cold without mercy;
Every seed will take root in the earth,
As the King of the elements desired
The braird will come forth with the dew,
It will inhale life from the soft wind.

I will come round with my step,
I will go rightways with the sun,
In name of Ariel and the angels nine,
In name of Gabriel and the Apostles kind.
Father, Son and Spirit Holy,
By giving growth and kindly substance
To every thing that is in my ground,
Till the day of gladness shall come.

The Feast day of Michael, day beneficent,
I will put my sickle round about
The root of my corn as was wont;
I will lift the first cut quickly;
I will put it three turns round
My head saying my rune the while,
My back to the airt of the north;
My face to the fair sun of power.

I shall throw the handful far from me,
I shall close my two eyes twice,
Should it fall in one bunch
My stacks will be productive and lasting;
No Carlin will come with bad times
To ask a palm bannock from us,
What time rough storms come with frowns
Nor stint nor hardship shall be on us.

A modern reader is struck by the closeness of man, the sower of seed, and God, the giver of life. This closeness is not simply a matter of prayer, as if a priest or holy man were blessing the work of the husbandman. The seedsman is his own priest; the work is equally labour and liturgy. It might seem that this liturgy is merely ornamental or simply a kind of offering and giving thanks. This it is, of course, for in this tradition Creation is a continuous gift and is, through all vicissitudes, received with thanksgiving, even when, and indeed especially when, nature is the bringer of adversity: drought or floods or disease.

But there is something else. Perhaps I can best express this by reference to a custom which I knew as a boy, a custom that has now disappeared with the disappearance of a certain way of life. It was the custom when one visited a house at the churning time of taking the churn-staff in one's hand and striking the cream with it a few times, thus helping the cream to break rightly and copiously into good butter. This simple neighbourly act had a lot of meaning and it would never have done to omit it. In the first place, it meant sharing in the work and the community created by this. Secondly, it meant a blessing on the home, either a substitute or an addition to the phrase which was never omitted by the visitor where any work was in progress: *Bail o Dhia ar an obair,* God's blessing on the work. Thirdly, and most basically, it meant the involvement of man and woman in the very process of Creation within which was seen the simple but very significant transformation of milk into cream into butter. The man who is going out to sow the seed is deeply involved in the processes of creation, as are the elements in a living active way.

> The shoot will come forth with the dew
> And will inhale life with the soft wind
>
> *Thig an Fochann leis an drúcht*
> *Geobhaidh se beatha on gaoith Ciúin*

Here we are at the living centre of the creative processes of nature, and man, the sower of seed, is intimately part of it. As he scatters the seed, aided by the wind, he walks in step with nature turning rightways *(deiseal)* with the sun. He is exactly situated in space and time in a world where each little field, each hillock and valley, has a name, and where not only each of the four seasons is noted but many lesser seasons as well, with each its own character and relationship to man's industry. This extends even to the days of the week, and, so, in the poem we are looking at, Friday is the best or most auspicious day for sowing the seed. This probably goes back to pre-Christian times, but, of course, in a Christian context, Friday is the day of the death and burial of Christ, the King of Friday, who is the seed of the new world of the Resurrection of man and nature.

As in the *Breastplate of St. Patrick* so, too, in this ancient prayer, the created world of the angels is given an essential and indeed a central place. An invisible world becomes present and, in its own way, visible. It is a hierarchical world, yet there is a strange democracy about it, and this comes out clearly in the third stanza of 'The Consecration of the Seed', where Father, Son and Holy Spirit arrive, as it were, in the midst of the angels. Elsewhere the Trinity is invoked as 'The Most Secret Three' (Carmichael, I, p.63) as if there were question of a hierarchy not of power but of spiritual inwardness.

The final two stanzas of 'The Consecration of the Seed' remind us how easily the world of the *Carmina* can be seen as a world tinged or imbued with superstition and a kind of magic. A certain ritual, altogether trivial in itself, is to be observed in order to call forth a good harvest and ensure protection against evil spirits. This attitude and these observances can indeed lose their living relationship with the tradition and the community, and become selfish and materialistic, but as they emerge within the tradition, and in full relationship with the spiritual world of purity and charity, they affirm our human involvement with the ongoing processes of creation, and with the great spiritual beings, the angels and archangels who are the companions and helpers of men and women.

There is also the Adversary, the Dark Powers named in the *Breastplate*, here appearing as 'the Carlin', Carmichael's translation of *An Caileach*, the old woman who comes to deceive and destroy, getting into the act, so to speak, by asking for a loaf of bread, and bringing with her a kind of blight and bad luck. The world of the *Carmina* is a world of brightness and goodness, and the poem we are looking at is typical of the relative importance accorded the good spirits and the evil forces. These latter come in on the fringe of things and cannot be ignored, but it is light and goodness and the Host of Heaven that dominate the landscape almost exactly as in the Lord's Prayer with its central movement to and from the Father in Heaven and its two final petitions dealing with the *peirasmos* of testing and the *ponéros* of destruction.

The *cailleach*, like the Morrigan, the Goddess of War, represents the devouring and destructive feminine, showing itself spectacularly in the figure of Sheila-na-Gig, at once menacing and inviting. All this negative feminine is of course balanced by the presence of Brigit and Mary, so present and powerful that the Saviour is named commonly as Mary's son, and the Easter cockcrow announces: The Son of the Virgin is victorious: *ta mac na h-óige slán*.

It must not be thought, however, that Mary, the Virgin, had as it were fulfilled her vocation by being the Mother of the Redeemer. Rather does Mary stand beside Jesus, not simply as Mother but, as in St. John's Gospel, as Woman and Consort: indeed the idea of co-redemption is quite near to the Celtic tradition in which nothing living or truly creative happens through seed-giving man that does not have its completion in the nurturing womb of the feminine.

8

COSMOGENESIS AND THE CELTIC IMAGINATION I

Teilhard de Chardin and George MacDonald

I. In Search of a New Design

The recovery or rediscovery of the Celtic world is the recovery or rediscovery of a certain way, varied and manifold yet identifiably one, of being human, of living and dying and relating to destiny and deity, to presence and presences. This means that that only is valid and valuable which is universally human, and finds some echo in every human mind and heart that seeks life and wholeness. This means, further, that what is recovered is also retrieved, in Heidegger's sense of being presented as a repeatable human possibility for wayfaring men and women. This means, finally, that what we identify as specially Celtic is to be found elsewhere, perhaps even more deeply and powerfully expressed in this or that individual instance, yet not found elsewhere to the same degree as a common characteristic of a whole civilisation, as a pervasive influence issuing from a deep common and ancient source.

It is not for antiquarian interest primarily that we look to our Celtic past and what remains of it today like coals under the 'smooring' that await a new kindling, but because the shape of our world is wrong and we are being wrongly shaped by it, as so many of our young people realise wildly and desperately. John Bate, a contemporary poet, has entitled a collection of his poems *Damaged Beauty Needs a New Design*, and the title could serve to describe what the retrieval of Celtic culture is all about.[27] We live in a world that is out of shape, and this world, beautiful indeed but damaged, desperately and urgently needs a new design. And if the vision that can create this design is not to be found in Celtic Christianity I do not know where it can be found.

What follows is not of course an attempt at providing this new design, but is rather concerned with a certain aspect of an imaginative vision that might, at whatever distance, serve to create it. To prepare the way for a new design is to enter into the mystery and sweep of what Pierre Teilhard de Chardin calls Cosmogenesis, and I shall begin by relating my personal pilgrimage to the place from which this strange, misunderstood prophet arose, and the discovery I made, entirely unexpectedly, as I made contact with that place.

II. A Casual Pilgrimage

In the summer of 1981 I spent a week in Clermont-Ferrand in the Auvergne district in South-East France. I was visiting friends, but part of my reason for being there was to visit the birth-place of Pierre Teilhard de Chardin, the controversial scientist-philosopher-theologian who came from nearby Sarcenat, and who spent some months every year during his pre-Jesuit days in Clermont-Ferrand itself. It was about that time that the centenary of Teilhard's birth had been celebrated; a stamp had been struck in his honour, and a small Paris street named after him.[28]

---

[27] *Damaged Beauty needs a new Design*, twenty poems by John Bate. Walter Ritchie, Kenilworth, Scotland, 1981. The verse that gives the book its title reads:
   In this tumbled present we must build,
   For damaged beauty needs a new design.
[28] It should be noted that French family names of the type of Teilhard de Chardin are properly abbreviated to the first part of the name: Teilhard de Chardin becomes commonly Teilhard, and I shall follow this usage.

I did not find the key I sought in Sarcenat nor in Clermont-Ferrand, but I found it nevertheless in that country among those mountains of the *massif central* from which this great prophet had come. But I did not know how to use that key, or indeed whether it served to open any door, until long after, when I read an almost totally unknown essay written over a hundred years ago by a Protestant minister from Aberdeen named George MacDonald.

Teilhard's best-known work is *The Phenomenon of Man*, first published in 1959 by William Collins of London, and Harper of New York, issued as a Fontana Paperback in 1965. The definitive French edition of Teilhard is published by Editions de Seuil (Paris), beginning with *Le Phénomène Humain* in 1955. Teilhard has been well served by his translators, yet in order to appreciate the rigour and depth of his thought it is necessary to consult the original. The standard French biography of Teilhard is that of Claude Cuénot, *Pierre Teilhard de Chardin, les grands étages de son évolution*, Paris, 1958 (English translation: *Teilhard de Chardin*, Burns and Oates, London, 1965). Robert Speaight's *Teilhard de Chardin: a Biography*, Collins, London, 1967, is a work of literature in its own right. The best general introduction to Teilhard's though is that of Emile Rideau, *La pensée de Teilhard de Chardin*, Paris, 1965 (English translation: *The Thought of Teilhard de Chardin*, New York, 1967). Donald Gray's *The One and the Many* (London, 1969) provides an excellent general summary of Teilhard's system. There are, however, two books especially which establish in a thoroughly scholarly and analytical way the greatness of Teilhard as a thinker. The first is *Bergson et Teilhard de Chardin* by Madeleine Barthélemy-Madaule, Editions de Seuil, Paris, 1963 (685 pp.) and the other is the more recent theological study of Teilhard by J. A. Lyons: *The Cosmic Christ in Origen and Teilhard de Chardin*, Oxford University Press, London, 1982. The first of these books places Teilhard within the central stream of Western philosophy and should have silenced those who attribute epistemological naïveté to Teilhard, if they have the resources to study it. The second, which comes with a foreword from Professor Wiles, places Teilhard's Cosmic Christology within one of the most profound traditions of Christian theology, a tradition that had come to be overlooked and marginalised in Teilhard's day.

III. George MacDonald's Defence of the Imagination

It was through G. K. Chesterton that I first became alerted to the significance of George MacDonald; it was through my colleague in the Faculty of Divinity of Edinburgh University, Professor John McIntyre, that I came to read MacDonald's essay on *Imagination* written in 1867.[29] Chesterton's essay first appeared as the *Introduction* to the biography of George MacDonald written by his son. It shows Chesterton, the literary critic, at his best, in seeing an author at the centre of his inspiration and in relation to the direction or 'intention' of his thought and aspiration. It places MacDonald in the context of Scottish Calvinism, and sees him as escaping from it by 'a miracle of imagination', so that in his fairy tales and novels we are able to see 'what Scottish religion would have been if it had continued the colour of medieval poetry'. MacDonald, for Chesterton, is a St. Francis of the North, 'who sees the same sort of halo round every flower and bird'.

[29] The full title of McDonald's essay is: *The Imagination, its Functions and its Culture*, and it first appeared in *A Dish of Orts*, George Newnes, London, 1905, pp. 1 to 42. Professor John McIntyre had included this essay in his special course on 'Theology and Human Imagination' which has been part of the Systematic Theology Honours Courses in the Faculty of Divinity of Edinburgh University for many years. The importance of imagination in theology is emphasised in a collection of papers edited by Professor J. P. Mackay of the same faculty as a festscript for Professor McIntyre (*Religious Imagination*, Edinburgh University press, 1986). Writing about MacDonald's essay Prof. McIntyre says: 'It is something of a classic in its own right, but though publication of it was delayed for some forty years it failed to produce any reaction in theological or other circles' (seminar notes, unpublished). Among the heirs of MacDonald there is not only Chesterton but also C. S. Lewis, J. R. R. Tolkien, and Charles Williams (see *The Inklings* by H. Carpenter, George Allen and Unwin, London, 1978). All references to MacDonald's essay refer to the pagination in *A Dish of Orts*. 'Orts' is a Scotticism meaning 'scraps', but in his preface the author makes it clear that he does not by any means 'associate the idea of worthlessness with the works contained in the book.'

MacDonald was a Scot from that most Scottish of cities, Aberdeen. Like Teilhard he came of a deeply Christian family, and like Teilhard he chose the Christian ministry as his vocation. Like Teilhard too, he found himself marginalised and 'out in the cold' among his co-religionists. But what is most striking is the parallel between these men and the cities and environs from which they came: Clermont-Ferrand and the Auvergne on the one hand, Aberdeen and the Eastern Highlands on the other. In both cases a fortress of ancient tradition had long settled into a kind of Gormenghast immobility among the hills. How could the human spirit escape from this unless by some kind of vertical take off as of a space rocket, by what Chesterton calls 'a miracle of imagination'. Perhaps I could push the rocket metaphor a little further and ask whether this strong gravitational pull may not be in all such cases necessary in order that the soaring imagination may travel deep into the realms of the intellectual heavens.

But we must go on to look at MacDonald's own understanding of imagination — it being clear by now that the key I sought in Clermont-Ferrand has to do with imagination, though there is something more, as will appear. Let us say that we have the material of the key, though not yet the final shape and make of it.

MacDonald's essay begins with 'a definition, or rather description' of the faculty to which we give the name of imagination. It is 'the faculty that gives form to thought' (p. 2), the kind of form which, whether uttered or not, is such that the senses can lay hold of the thought by way of it. And here MacDonald, for whom lateral thinking was second nature, swings his definition or description into that orbit where it circles throughout the whole essay. Man himself, he tells us, bodies forth the thought of God, because creation is an exercise of divine imagination. So it is that 'the imagination of man is made to the image of the imagination of God' (p. 3). We have here a very bold and original application of the Genesis statement that God made man in his own image and likeness. It centres the image neither in man's intellect nor in his aspiration but in his imagination, as the power of giving form and embodiment to thought and aspiration. This is not to say that the image is absent (for MacDonald) from the intellectual and the aspirational side of men and women, but only that it is found primarily and, as it were, with its special hallmark, in the imagination. Elsewhere, in his talk on Wordsworth, he tells us that while nature proceeds from the imagination of God, man proceeds from the love of God (p. 254). Indeed, both in God's creation and in human creativity MacDonald sees imagination as the servant not only of love but of thought. (p. 3). This is an important point. MacDonald is able to release the imagination and allow it to move freely and easily through all the regions of knowledge — science, history, philosophy and theology as well as poetry — only because he has already, like a good horseman, learned when to give it its head and when to rein it in. And if thought, intellect, consistent logical reflection provides the reins, it can be said that observation provides the highways and byways of its journeying. But at this point the metaphor becomes a little strained, for there is a sense in which imagination discovers its own pathways, creates its own regions to explore: Lilliput, Erewhon, Narnia, Middle-earth, etc. Yet here most of all the hand on the rein must be as firm as it is light, so that the imaginary world is formed according to the shapes and colours of the world of observation. The wonders of any possible wonderland are wonderful only in relation to the world of everyday observation.

For it must be realised that, like every other human power and skill, the imagination has its diseases and distortions, its abuses and misuses. It is possible to speak of a demonic imagination, which shows itself in tyrants and torturers and in some writers of fantasy. There is the pornographic imagination, that takes sexuality out of its proper setting in human life and human love, and so destroys it. There is, to return to the normal human sphere, the day-dreaming imagination, which serves a purpose in our early years but can, if not transcended, become a substitute for living and a way of escaping from reality. There is the 'Micawber' imagination always 'waiting for something to turn up', and thus excusing its possessor from looking at the plain economic facts of life. There is, and this is very common and very distressing if not destructive, the worrier's imagination which goes in the opposite direction to that of Mr Micawber, and is always expecting something catastrophic to turn up. The list could be lengthened, but enough has been said to make it clear that imagination, if it becomes separated from common observation and commonsense, on the one hand, or from the pursuit of truth and goodness on the other, can diminish or destroy the image of God in man and woman.

George MacDonald allowed for this *caveat*, but he did not spell it out. He was more concerned with rescuing imagination from its prison in the frontiers of orthodoxy and allowing it its proper and necessary freedom. Of course the poet was always allowed into the prison precincts to ride this imprisoned Pegasus at will, but then the poet and his winged steed had no place among the scientists, historians, philosophers and theologians except perhaps as a kind of decorative extra. What MacDonald (and those who agree with him, in ancient or modern times) claims is that it is imagination that is the proper leader of all human enterprises, though it must be directed and corrected by thought and observation. 'Directed' is perhaps too strong a word, for it is imagination that opens the way forward, that has a vision of things new and a remembrance of things past, that truly leads the way, but it must always keep in touch with its sober and hardworking brothers: observation and thought. This metaphor of the family is in fact MacDonald's, and it is interesting that within this metaphor imagination is feminine, sister to those two earthbound brothers. The three must travel together, but imagination leads the way, and sheds its light on the journey ahead.

Imagination is the discoverer of the new, that which leads us forward on the road of becoming, of evolution, of genesis. Already we are in sight of Teilhard and Cosmogenesis. We have perhaps had a glimpse of the key to Teilhard, as we think of that self-enclosed chateau of Sarcenat, of the bourgeois solidity and heaviness of Clermont-Ferrand (as of MacDonald's Aberdeen) and see, in a moment of imagination, that upsurge, that escape, that affirmation of a new world, that great and dazzling light that issued forth from that closed and enclosing place at a time when the world seemed to have renounced all sense of its own future, all vision of a world in the making

IV. Teilhard's Vision

As I read MacDonald's essay it became clear to see that here was/is the key to the phenomenon of Teilhard. And then I realised that this key was already in my hand, that like the golden key of the same MacDonald's fairytale I had found it long before I quite knew what to do with it, what door it unlocked. I had found the key not in Sarcenat nor in Clermont-Ferrand but in a place called Gergovie nearby, where on an elevation or plateau there is a memorial to Vercingetorix. Here at Gergovia — the name has remained — the Celts of Gaul had defeated Caesar, only to be defeated later when Vercingetorix was captured, imprisoned and cruelly slain.

So this, I realised, was Celtic country, in which the past is remembered even when, as in the Highlands of Scotland, that past has defeat and subjection at the heart of it.[30] I knew that

---

[30] It is only recently that French historians are coming to recognise the continuing presence and relevance of their Celtic origins. See *Les Gaulois* by Regine Pernoud. Paris: Editions de Seuil, 1979.

Teilhard was deeply attached to this country from which he had come, and I asked myself whether it is my own Celtic imagination, moving ahead too quickly, that had caught a familiar trick of countenance in the many photographs we have of Teilhard, familiar to me in the faces of the mountainy men of Kerry in the south-west of Ireland. But let this pass for fancy, even though the observation preceded the discovery of the Celtic connection. Let us look rather at the work of Teilhard as the creation of a certain kind of imagination.

Teilhard was at once a man of the earth and a man of God, and his whole life was a continual study of, alternatively and together, the one and the other: geology and palaeontology on the one hand, and philosophy and theology on the other. On both sides he made valuable contributions to knowledge, but his unique and enduring achievement is to have brought earth and heaven together in a bold, imaginative, and deeply realised synthesis, deeply realised in the sense that it took account of all the facts and faced all the difficulties, theoretical and practical, involved in this great enterprise. As in every imaginative thinker there is an underlying tension all the way between image and observation, but Teilhard never allows the image to free itself from the demands of observation.

This is not the place to attempt a full statement, even in summary fashion, of Teilhard's cosmological synthesis. But I want to look briefly at his main images or 'imaginations', which are like the winged horses of fable that unite earth and heaven. These are: radial energy, point Omega, complexity-consciousness, Cosmogenesis. Radial energy expresses, in physical terms, the ancient principle, which goes back to the pre-Socratic physical philosophers, that everything is in everything. But Teilhard transforms a static principle into an active principle: everything, each individual atom or monad, has within it a force or energy by which it goes beyond itself towards cosmic unity. This force cannot be directly observed any more than the kinetic and potential energies of classical mechanics can be directly observed. But it differs from these and other scientific concepts in not being physically measurable or quantifiable. It is an imagination or imaginative construct, and in this it is no different from other conceptions used by physicists and other scientists. Until quite recently, however, the fact that these constructs are imaginary was obscured by the fact that 'exact' measurements would be attached to them: it was not generally seen that all that could be said with factual accuracy is that we are able to apply certain processes of measurement to the physical world. Yet scientists nevertheless use their imaginations to build up a vision of the physical world without which science could not function. Measurement, experiment, and the rest serve as a negative check, a kind of anchorage for imagination, or better, a viewpoint whence visions open up towards near or far horizons. Now Teilhard was a most painstaking scientist, highly respected by his fellow scientists in the field of palaeontology and he remained all his life ready to be judged by the negative criterion of factual observation and careful measurement. But he was blessed (and burdened) by a holistic imagination of unique power and demandingness, holistic in the sense that no partial vision, no near horizon, no incomplete 'story' could satisfy him. It was this passionate search for unity and completeness that generated this primary 'imagination' which he termed radial energy. It is the energy of unification, by which each particle radiates towards its fellows under the universal attraction of point Omega.

But before looking at this central and centering conception or imagination which Teilhard names Omega it is necessary to bring up a principle that lies near the centre of Teilhard's vision — though it is rarely brought to the centre of his expositions: the principle that 'union differentiates'. This means that when two things unite to form one thing, or more correctly to form one community, then each by this union and communion becomes more fully and 'differently' itself. Thus, in a good marriage the man becomes more fully man and the woman more fully woman; in any community of persons community is enhanced by the variety of persons who compose it. So it is that radial energy does not result in a dead uniformity of aggregation but in an ever deepening harmony in variety, in which each entity performs in its special way, discovers its voice, as it were, and fulfils its deepest instincts. Teilhard is here very near to the ancient Greek imagination of 'the breathing-together of all things', and not far from the Platonic and Neoplatonic conception of a world-soul: indeed, as we shall see, he gives these conceptions a profound Christian significance.

What then is Omega? Concretely it is at once God, Christ, the End of the World, the fulfilment of the whole great enterprise of creation. It is what Alfred Tennyson called 'that far-off divine event towards which the whole creation moves'; more prosaically it is what the Americans call 'the bottom line'. Most usually Teilhard sees it as the *Pleroma*, that ultimate state of the world in which all differences are reconciled, in which, in accordance with the principle that 'union differentiates', every single atom and event within the length and breadth of time and space finds its place and significance. Always all and everything is in movement towards this end, that is not only fulfilment but also a new beginning. God is at once present within this process, and is also calling it onwards towards himself. God is not simply above and beyond the human and created world; he is ahead of it, leading it onwards, and also within it as its ambience or milieu.

And so we come to the central concept of Cosmogenesis — with its attendant concepts of Noogenesis and Christogenesis. Contrary to what is generally assumed, especially by critics of Teilhard, Cosmogenesis does not depend on theories, whether of the Darwinian or Lamarckian varieties, though Teilhard makes frequent use of the terms and concepts used by both types of evolutionary theorists. In Cosmogenesis the accent is on 'cosmo' rather than 'genesis'. What Teilhard is saying is that every atom of the universe is saturated with order, that every least event reflects the whole vast enterprise: so he can say that 'the mesh of the universe is the universe itself'. This reflexivity, this mirroring of the whole in the part, reaches a certain threshold of intensity in man, in the emergence of mind (Noogenesis), and in Christ this mirroring becomes total, so that the universe flames forth a kind of conflagration of light and fire. For the original radiance of radial energy is not a simple representation but is also, even more fundamentally, an orientation, a seeking and questing which is the first stirrings of that love which in Christ becomes the 'amorisation' of the universe.

Now of course Teilhard shares this vision of final unity and 'homecoming' with many philosophers, poets and mystics: Plotinus, Dante, Descartes, Eckhart, etc. But in all these visionaries the material world is transcended, ignored, placed in brackets, at best reduced to a subordinate place. Only in Teilhard does every least particle reflect all the radiance of heaven; only in Teilhard does the body of Christ become not only bread but stone, so that the Eucharist reveals a physical world in process of total transubstantiation; only in Teilhard do we find a conception, an 'imagination', that takes the weight and strain of all the heaviness, grossness and intractability of matter and the physical. Not only the forms of nature in their beauty and variety (as in Wordsworth, for example) but that material substrate which underlies them in their constant generation and corruption.

There is a world within the world or beneath the world, a hypogeum, a place of darkness, terror and aloneness, an alien place ruled by an alien power from which human imagination has always turned back, and into which Teilhard took his vision of light and life, and asks us to follow him. This is the world of the Dragon, this is the place of the Dragon, this we must look at steadily if we are to understand Teilhard's enterprise and its relationship to the Celtic imagination and to that new design which our world so desperately and despairingly needs.

V. The Dragon

The Dragon is already there in the Old Testament, as the original void and darkness of Genesis; as the dark waters of the psalmist, those depths out of which man comes to God; as the Monster of the Deep that swallows Jonas; as the Leviathan of Job; as Sheol, alien and cold and full of shadows. The relationship of the Dragon to the God of Abraham and Isaac and Jacob is ambiguous and problematical: at times the Adversary of God as of man, at times the servant of God, at times an aspect of God. And then something new comes in with Isaiah: the Suffering Servant, who confronts the Dragon by obedience and suffering, and so wins a strange victory.

In the New Testament the Dragon is Satan, called also the Adversary, the Evil One *(Ponéros)*, the Prince of this world, the Lord of Death, the one who sifts and tests. Finally, the Dragon is named *as* the Dragon, and given imaginative shape and form as he/it confronts the child of the Woman and the great angel Michael, in the Book of Revelation. Again in the New Testament, the relationship of the Dragon to the Father-God is ambiguous, being variously enemy and alien, and, on the other hand, servant. Clearly the whole of the New Testament, the Four Gospels especially, is governed by the vision of Isaiah: Jesus, the Lord's anointed, is the sacrificial Lamb, the Suffering Servant who defeats the Dragon by obedience and suffering, who goes down into the world of death, into the darkness of the nether regions, and breaks forth triumphantly from the prison of death, from the House of the Dragon. But the condition for this victory, for this rising up, is the defeat and going down by the bitter death on the cross where the Lord's anointed is spared neither pain nor humiliation nor dereliction.

The first Christians knew that the Dragon was defeated, and they were convinced that this victory would very soon manifest itself on a cosmic scale when Jesus would descend in glory (just as he had ascended) to judge the living and the dead. We still await this mighty event after two thousand years, and the Dragon is still with us, more powerful and menacing, it would seem, than ever before.

The Dragon is present in many shapes and forms, and is variously named in all religions and philosophical traditions, including that religio-philosophical tradition which, with Christianity, as created the modern world. There was a great deal of dualism in the Greek tradition, and it influenced both the tragic and philosophical views of man. But in any case that mighty eruption of human self-consciousness which took place in fifth and fourth century Athens had its own special awareness of the Dragon. For the great tragedians — Aeschylus, Sophocles and Euripides — the Dragon was that Fate or Necessity which lay in wait for the tragic hero, and awakened pity and terror in the audience, which thus found a way of coping with the Dragon, accepting its power, and keeping, by comparison with the hero, a very low profile. In the background is the doomed Homeric hero: Hector, Achilles and the rest — only the modest and circumspect Ulysses escapes.

The philosophers, at least after Socrates, escaped from the Dragon by focusing their whole attention on an intelligible reality beyond the world (Plato) or within it (Aristotle), so that the Dragon was placed in the shadows and indeed made to mingle with the shadows. For Plato matter is less than wholly real, for Aristotle matter is a primordial shapeless substratum of change and transformation, and it is always attended by the shadowy presence of *sterésis*, privation, which in the resolution of the problem of change, identified so sharply by the Eleatics, is even more important than matter. Contrary to what is commonly assumed by apologists of Christianity, the Greeks did not deny the reality of the material world. What they did was to strive to bring it to heel, to dominate it, to reduce its wild and terrifying irrationality to rational terms. This process culminated in the elegant and comprehensive hierarchical system of Plotinus, who by way of Augustine, was to provide Christianity with its basic vision of good and evil for over a thousand years. What Augustine found in Plotinus was the vision of a 'light above the mind' of such power and radiance that it penetrated into the very depths of the material world, and set to flight all the shadows that seemed to form a substantial alternative and contrary reality over against the divine goodness. Matter exists, yes, but the evil attendant on matter, and man's immersion in matter, has no substance whatsoever, does not exist at all.

What St. Augustine thus describes, in the tenth chapter of the seventh book of his *Confessions*, is surely one of the great dramatic moments in the history of Christian thought. Already Augustine has rejected the position that there is no such thing as evil 'for even if this is so the very fact that we fear evil is itself an evil'. Yet what he discovered by reading Plotinus is that evil does not exist as an entity or substance. It is merely a privation: Aristotle's shadow-attached-to-matter now takes the place of matter. And this shadow disappears under the light from the Source. That is what Augustine saw in one moment of total realisation. As long as he could look steadily at the Source, evil vanished into nothingness. It was this metaphysics of good and evil that Aquinas took over, and that still remains the basic teaching of Catholic Christianity. It was the metaphysical theory that Teilhard imbibed in his student days. *Omne ens est bonum*, he learned: all that is, is good; evil simply is not.

This amazing principle, totally and radically optimistic, might be called the motto or device of scholasticism, and it is the foundation of Teilhard's cosmic philosophy. Yet it went hand in hand with the ancient and medieval doctrine of hell and eternal damnation, and no metaphysical distancing or dismissal of evil could diminish the ever-present menace and terror of this adamantine reality, this vision of a kingdom where the Dragon, in his banishment from earth, had total and everlasting power. This Prince of Darkness was present everywhere on earth as tempter and unsleeping adversary. Moreover, the whole world of matter, even the world of living nature, was so deeply occupied by the Dragon and his minions that, in the ancient Blessing of Lustral or 'Holy' water, the priest began by exorcising the water and the salt. The Divine Office contained, and to a lesser extent still contains, a continuous recognition of the presence and power of the Dragon who 'goes about like a roaring lion seeking whom he may devour': the warning from *Peter* sounds even more fearsome and awesome in the ancient sonorous Latin: *sicut leo rugiens circuit, quarens quem devoret.* Teilhard heard these words every day, or at least read them in reading his breviary, and he knew well that the earth (and the elements of the earth) was seen as the Place of the Dragon, not itself evil but nevertheless, to use C. S. Lewis's phrase, 'occupied territory'. The lover of God looked beyond this territory, beyond this *vallis lacrimarum* to the heavenly kingdom. To love the earth and the things of the earth was to enter the Dragon's mouth and be devoured.

Now, Teilhard's most profound and radical decision was that of fully accepting 'the world', the cosmos for which Christ did *not* pray (John 17.9). This was the theme of his first book *Le Milieu Divin*, and this is clearly and forcefully stated in the dedication of *The Phenomenon of Man* 'to those who love the world'. It is clear, moreover, that 'the old Dragon underground' begins to vanish for Teilhard, so that he comes to adopt a purely formal doctrine of hell as a mere possibility: 'the roaring lion' has become a chimera. The *omne ens est bonum* principle of the neoplatonic Augustine has triumphed over the pessimistic anti-humanism of the later Augustine.

For Teilhard, then, all that is is good and all that is, *nothing excluded,* is involved in the ultimate home-coming at point Omega. As for Dante, all things are infolded, gathered in, all the scattered leaves of the universe, but, unlike Dante, Teilhard does not envisage an *inferno* populated with the enemies of God (and of Dante!) and ruled over by the Dragon. The Cosmic Dragon has been absorbed into the process of Cosmogenesis.

This has enormous practical consequences. It means the acceptance of technology and the whole scientific enterprise, something that Teilhard's contemporary, Gabriel Marcel, saw as totally outrageous, a kind of promethean pride and blindness. And there is no doubt but that some of the wisest of Teilhard's contemporaries, not only Marcel but other genuine prophetical thinkers, such as Nicholas Berdyaev and G. K. Chesterton, either could or would have found Teilhard's position totally unacceptable, and indeed extremely dangerous. Yet some of the mystics would have understood: Julian of Norwich, for instance, or Thérèse of Lisieux. In our own day another woman mystic, Adrienne von Speyr, has persuaded one of our leading Catholic theologians, Hans Urs von Balthasar, in the same direction. Thinking of Teilhard's deep and creative relationships with women one wonders whether this homecoming of the Dragon (created after all by God in Christ) may not be heralded by women, and ultimately by the Woman who, from *Genesis* to *Revelation,* is the enemy of the Dragon, whose head she will crush. But I cannot explore this Marian horizon here, beyond noting Teilhard's openness to the influence of the feminine, as he sought to conquer that 'old dragon underground' and bring it within the mighty creative processes of Cosmogenesis and Christogenesis.

VI. The Hypogeum

Some years ago I had the experience of descending into one of those ancient burial chambers in Malta called hypogeums or hypogea. It was not particularly deep or terrifying, though I felt that slight panic which many people feel in such deep closed-in places. But Malta is a place of ancient temples of the Mother-God, and it has deep prehistoric links with this same cult in my own country of South-West Ireland, Slievenamon, and the Paps of Dana. The whole experience of the temples and the hypogeum brought up in me ancient terrors and the challenge that goes with these terrors, the challenge of facing them and outfacing them. It was imagination that had brought me into this world of living death, the archetypal 'burial alive' of Jonas, and the mysticism of the Dark Night of the Spirit, that choking terror in which the human spirit quails and breaks. As imagination brought me there, so imagination could easily bring me back, could allow me to escape. But in that case I was neither facing the terror nor outfacing it. And there was a deep but real sense in which I was forsaking my fellow men, my brothers and sisters, who were held captive in this eternal and infinite bondage. Another kind of imagination was necessary in order that I might go forward into this darkness and terror. I had to find the *meaning* of it all; I had to bring the strong light of universal intelligence to bear on it, to bring light into the darkness.

But what if the Dark has the last word? What if the Dragon is to rule for ever in its underground kingdom? Must I not at all costs escape from that? My brothers and sisters are doomed; they are lost, the damned, the unregenerate, the God-forsaken. Let me quickly return to the light above the ground and gain some credit, by faith or works or both, with the God of Justice and Wrath who will banish me to this everlasting living death unless I find favour with Him. This has been the way of many Christians over the centuries. They admit indeed that Jesus Christ descended into Hell, or some region of hell ('not the hell of the damned', the old Catechism used to say) but he came back again and left the netherworld to everlasting darkness, terror and pain. Indeed, mystics over the centuries, including that very practical and human woman, Teresa of Avila, have had visions of this terrible region, and have seen it as beyond redemption, beyond hope. *Lasciate ogni speranza*, 'abandon all hope who enter here' is written over its dreadful gateway, in Dante's vision.

Now if we are to take seriously the traditional Christian metaphysics of evil, *omne ens est bonum* (all that is, is good) then this all too real hypocosmic region must be seen as good. And indeed Christian theologians have done their best to see it as somehow 'fitting in', and some (including Thomas Aquinas and Bonaventure) have seen the contemplation of the sufferings of the Damned as part of the beatitude of the Justified. In this theology it seems to me that the Dragon has succeeded in hiding in the face of God. So Hell and the World of the Dragon is at once real and good because it has found a place in Heaven and God's purposes. The dark shadow of Vindicative Justice has shrouded the Face of Eternal Love and Mercy.

All this, both in its theological and mystical aspects, may be called the Night Imagination of Christianity as it has developed over the centuries. Its strength and reasonableness lies in this, that it takes seriously the Mystery of Iniquity, and the responsibility of both angelic and human spirits to create their own world. In our own day Karl Barth and others have tended towards a kind of Universalism or Salvation for all, in which this freedom is sacrificed to the universal saving will of God in Christ. This is the Despotism of Good and the disappearance of man's/woman's responsibility for their ultimate destiny. It issues in a deterministic cosmology. Yet it must be noted, all the same, that this is not far from Mother Julian's conception of a Great Deed by which 'all manner of things will be well'. Perhaps Mother Julian was a forerunner of what was/is deepest and best in Reform Theology.

Teilhard never, as far as I know, used the term 'Universalism', but it is clear that he believed in Universal Salvation. However, his approach to it, unconscious up to a point, is not by way of theological or mystical imagination but by way of scientific imagination. What he understood was that the stones which he loved so much from his earliest years had something to say, and that it was for him to report their message to men and angels. Of course the stones stood for the whole material world, not just the living world of nature but that dead subworld, terranean and subterranean, by which the living world had its density and physical substantiality. This is the world of the Dragon, of the hypogeum, of the mountain that cast the shadow of fear over the youthful Wordsworth, of Byron's dark and uncontrollable ocean. Teilhard saw it as a world waiting to tell its meaning, and this meaning both revealed Christ and revealed itself through Christ.

It has been said that Teilhard was 'a man of old stones and old bones', and indeed he became a highly skilled amateur geologist and a highly respected professional palaeontologist. But what is unique about his life and work is the way the stones and bones came alive under the living sunlight of his imagination. All his central concepts — radial energy, Omega, complexity-consciousness, Hominisation, Cosmogenesis, Christogenesis — were rays of this vital and vitalising sunlight. This illuminative power penetrated to the very depths of matter, and was strong enough to transfuse the world of advanced technology, even as far as nuclear technology. Everything found a place within the vast sweep of this centering vision, in which union not only unified but differentiated the vast multiplicity held in the womb of Time as it travelled through Space, as Mary travelled from Nazareth to Judaea carrying the Christ within her. Teilhard did not use the comparison, yet it is totally apt in an account of his vision, for all cosmic becoming is equally 'Christic' becoming: every least particle is held together by One who descended into the depths to raise up the whole cosmos in the universal transformation of the Resurrection and Ascension.

But Christ descended further still; descended into hell, and there too Teilhard's imagination follows him. In the logic of Teilhard's position the Christic — *le Cristique* — penetrates the very depths of the underworld so that nothing is left behind, nothing is relinquished. Hell is, in von Balthasar's words, 'a Christological place'. Not that Teilhard made this affirmation in so many words, but it is implicit in his Cosmic Christology and in his radical option for matter and the immensities of 'Chaos and Old Night'. This is the world of the Jonas experience, of the hypogeum and the taste of death. It is also the world of Gethsemane and the *Lamma Sabacthani*, the absence of God and of all life and light. It is the place of the mystical Dark Night of the Spirit, described with unique power and clarity by St. John of the Cross. It is the place of those 'anxieties' that returned again and again to trouble Teilhard in his later years. It is the place of panic and terror, a sweating terror that begins to turn to blood. It is here especially we feel the literal truth of Teilhard's claim, that it was through his deep union of prayer with his house-bound invalid sister that he fulfilled his vocation as an explorer of new realms of understanding. In the end it had to be the Woman who made it possible to outface the Dragon and make *all* things captive to Christ.

Teilhard's creative and illuminating imagination always moved ahead of observation, and also of theoretical and logical demonstration, yet it never loses them; they are always in sight. He is always ready to check his vision against any new observation or theories that science provides; at the theological level he remains a Catholic Christian even though he pushes very strongly at the limits of the orthodoxy of his time, and indeed helped to create the very different world of Vatican II. Yet it must be admitted, indeed affirmed, that his imagination does move forward, and that the world of his imagination opens out towards new horizons, and may well mistake at times the contours of these horizons. This is especially true in what I have described as his encounter with the Dragon. All we can expect of him is a glimpse or glimpses of possible horizons, a first rough (and corrigible) sketch of a new design.

9

COSMOGENESIS AND THE CELTIC IMAGINATION II

The Cosmic Presences

I. Science and Imagination

I have said that it was at Gergovie, with its memorial of the far Celtic past, that I found the key to the vision of Pierre Teilhard de Chardin. That key was and is Imagination as described by MacDonald, that Celtic imagination which the Protestant minister from Aberdeen shared with the Jesuit priest from Clermont-Ferrand. As I began by saying, whatever of universal value is found in that hidden ancient world now revealing itself must be itself something universally human, something special to that world only by emphasis and accentuation. In this sense, and only in this sense, the Celtic imagination is a power and a glory to be revealed; a power and a glory which has indeed shone forth in Teilhard as it shone forth in Scotus Eriugena in the ninth century, and in the 'Subtle Doctor' from Duns in the thirteenth.

But this glory of imagination, this fount of vision, has its source in an ancient way of being, with its customs and languages, its feel for life, its pathos and poetry, even in the shadows attendant on its human limitations. And it is this Source-vision, this special expression of the Divine Imagination, that I want to recover as a key to the understanding of Teilhard's great vision that unites heaven and earth and the dark region under the earth, so that 'at the name of Jesus every knee should bow, in heaven and on earth and under the earth' (Phil. 2.11).

The Celtic way of being is first and last a way of seeing, a vision. Vision is, of course, at the centre of all poetry, all philosophy, all religious experience, yet Celtic poetry, whose birth is the birth of European 'vernacular' literature, and whose voice still echoes at the margins of Western Christendom, is bathed in a light that not only touches the surfaces of things but goes *into* things, penetrates the immediate shapes and colours, and celebrates what Kathleen Raine — herself a poet in this tradition — calls 'the mountain behind the mountain; what the eye of the seer glimpses behind the appearances of common day. It is the vision of a way of being that is always *en route,* always faring forward, always glimpsing at the horizon's edge the light of other worlds. There is a sense in which Europe is the creation of those Celtic monks who went forth from the Isles of the North to conquer a world of darkness, for the light that troubled their dreams had to shine *into* the darkness: it was a Christian light, incarnate, sacrificial. It was a light and a vision that had been tested and purified and deepened in the darkness of Gethsemane and Calvary, a light breaking forth from the Cross, an Easter light, a vision of the Risen Lord who was 'the Son of the gentle Mary'.

There is in this Celtic visionary tradition a kind of 'excess of light' which more prosaic and pedantic people find disconcerting, and in some cases totally unacceptable. Strangely, it has generated totally uncritical and unscholarly dismissals of Teilhard's visionary enterprise on the part of certain dons and *savants* such as P. B. Medawar and Jacques Monod: both make the curious logical mistake of assuming that, because the author they are criticising seems *to them* to be pretentious and rhetorical, he can therefore be dismissed in a few pretentious and rhetorical phrases: yet it is this dismissal that had to be substantiated by precise and careful analysis.[31] It is because the

---

[31]P. B. Medawar's 'emotional invective' (to use C. E. Raven's description of it in his book on Teilhard, Collins, 1962, p. 19) appeared in *Mind*, LXX, no. 272; Jacques Monod's dismissal will be found in *Chance and Necessity*, Collins, 1974, p. 19.

systematic never overcomes the visionary in Teilhard that it comes to be assumed that there is only the visionary, the dance of imagination leading ahead. It is true that this kind of visionary imagination turns easily to celebration, but it is normally quite conscious of this, as in the case for instance of James Joyce and George Bernard Shaw. Shaw it was who had pointed out, in *John Bull's Other Island*, that your typical Irishman (or woman) is severely practical, and indeed unromantic in everyday affairs no matter what visions may sustain or trouble them.

Yet to invoke James Joyce is to be forced to recognise the darker side of the Celtic imagination, and of course this sombre side of Joyce has been powerfully developed by Samuel Beckett. There is here a kind of crossroads or watershed of which George MacDonald was deeply conscious. There is much in human experience that can lead the human imagination towards darkness and despair, as indeed Teilhard, with his recurrent bouts of 'anxiety', well knew.[32] But it is at this point that for both Teilhard and MacDonald, the light of faith illuminates the darkness *from within*. It is this ultimate decision, without foundation except in itself, that renders Teilhard unforgivably romantic and unscientific for some of his critics: they do not see that they have made their own (negative) decision at this point. Here is how MacDonald describes this fundamental option: 'Through the combined lenses of science and imagination, we look back into ancient times, so dreadful in their incompleteness, that it may well have been the task of seraphic faith, as well as of cherubic imagination, to behold in the wallowing monstrosities of terror-seeming earth, the prospective, quiet, age-long labour of God preparing the world with all its humble graceful service for unborn man'. On the one hand dark images of turmoil and despair, on the other

[32] See Speaight, p. 260.

soaring images of genesis and transformation: there is no third option, as Teilhard shows clearly in one of his most remarkable essays, *Turmoil or Genesis,* using with almost unexampled power 'the combined lenses of science and imagination'. The Medawars and Monods of this world find this combination scandalous, yet it is clear that they too employ imagination, albeit in a narrow and blinkered fashion; indeed, as MacDonald points out, all scientific discovery comes by way of imagination, though it can lose this vital glow as it is tested and 'proved' under the cold light of the laboratory. What Teilhard does is to recover and deepen and extend in great rings of light that original glow. That is why every sentence he wrote is full of the excitement of discovery.

In the passage just quoted from MacDonald there is no mistaking the presence of the Dragon, clearly set in opposition to the angelic hierarchies, the Seraphim of faith and the Cherubim of imagination. This recognition of a Spirit-World is central to Celtic cosmology and Celtic imagination. Michael, Gabriel, Raphael, Ariel, Uriel are again and again invoked as protective powers in the face of destructive and seductive powers of darkness. The angelic powers do not destroy the demonic; rather are they both servants of the continuing manifestation of the designs of the Creator.

It would seem at first sight that these cosmic powers are entirely absent from the thought-world of Teilhard. There is a sense in which he writes within the scientific milieu; however daringly he 'takes off', he always returns to this world and its admissible limits of discourse. In any case he will not admit a dualism of the material-demonic and the angelic-spiritual. His fundamental option is that of total acceptance of the material in all its naked materiality. The world cannot shed its matter like a corpse in any hoped-for Parousia or End-Time, for corporeality itself is radiant with radial energy. There is no cut-off point between the earth and the realm under the earth, no place for Sheol or Hades or limbo or hell. Purgatory, yes emphatically, for Purgatory is traditionally understood in terms of genesis and transformation. Neither above nor below is there break and discontinuity. Christ, *Le Christique,* fills the whole created world, holding all things together so that God is in all.

Nevertheless Teilhard's world is incomplete without the presence of those cosmic spirit-beings which are already so vividly and deeply present in that same Celtic world which has such deep affinity with his own Cosmic imagination. This world needs his vision as he in turn needs this world's vision, as I shall try to show.

II. The Angels

I have been saying that it was in the discovery of Celtic Auvergne that I found the key to the thought-world or imagination-world of Teilhard de Chardin, and I have brought up certain considerations of a persuasive or rhetorical nature in favour of this connection. But I am very far from claiming that this imaginative discovery of mine keeps sufficiently close to the facts of Teilhard's life and milieu to allow it to be brought under what MacDonald calls the 'lens of science'. It must remain a personal discovery with some slight claim to become a public hypothesis. Its main function in this exploration has been to open up the possibility of bringing together Teilhard's cosmic vision and the world of Celtic inner vision, in order to offer a preliminary sketch or possible programme for the damaged beauty of the Christian world. At this point I want to look at this vision in itself.[33]

---

[33] See N. D. O'Donoghue, *The Holy Mountain* (The Liturgical Press, Collegeville, Minnesota, 1983) ch. 9: 'The Place of the Angels'. This is largely based on Carmichael's *Carmina Gadelica.*

The Celtic cosmic vision is centred on a vision of 'cosmic persons' or angels who are the guardians of all that is true and beautiful in the world, and to whose presence and power we naturally look for light and guidance in shaping our new design. This is not an antiquarian investigation, but the vital question of the validity of this vision, its place in a comprehensive theology, and its availability to contemporary men and women. I shall try to meet each of these points in turn.

A The question of validity, considered within a purely Christian context, becomes essentially a question of Scriptural warrant. And of course there is abundance of this. Neither in the Old nor in the New Testament writings is God alone in the heavens. In the Old Testament He is *Jahweh Sabaoth,* the One Who is surrounded by a vast multitude of beings who are real, each in its own measure of existence *and operation.* In medieval philosophy it was agreed among all the contending schools that existence and operation, or activity, belong indissolubly together. So it would have been a contradiction in terms to conceive of a region of cosmic or angelic powers who did not have a range of activity commensurate with their greatness. This principle is implied in the Old Testament and in the New. The angels are indeed messengers who in Milton's phrase 'stand and wait', but they are, as man is, though much more powerfully than man, makers and shapers of the heavens and the earth. Moreover, these beings are free, and some have turned away from their Centre and Source and are Fallen Angels. These have not lost their essential nature, and so remain active and powerful. At this point certain Gnostic Christians, as well as the followers of Manes, who revived the ancient Persian Dualism, saw the earth as the creation of a fallen angel or angels. Mainstream Christian theology rejected this (as did Neo-Platonism), but the presence and activity of these cosmic forces was never in question: it is indeed at the very centre of the New Testament story of redemption. For example what is called the priestly prayer of Jesus (in John 17) is in one of its main aspects a protection-prayer against the Evil One (*Ponéros*) and the forces that rule the 'world' (*cosmos*); and of course protection-prayers have large place in Celtic hymns and invocations, as we have seen.

It may be further noted that these Fallen Angels or 'Demons' are sometimes seen as divine messengers with permission or even commission from God to test or to destroy. If we examine carefully the attitude of Jesus to these entities in the Synoptic Gospels, in *Mark* especially, we realise that he does not call down destruction on these beings, but rather puts them in their allotted place: this is the force of the verb *epitimao*, sometimes translated 'rebuke'. Indeed the *Epistle of Jude* makes this point explicitly: the demons must be treated with respect and rebuked only by God, to Whom we can make appeal that *He* should rebuke them.

It is over against the presence and power of the Fallen Angels that we can best form an idea of the presence and power of what are called the Angels of God. These too can be sent on missions of purification or destruction, but essentially they are the friends of man and woman, powerful and ever-present friends whose help can be prayed for, and whose presence can at times be clearly felt or perceived. It is through them that the Law was given to the Jews (Gal. 3.19); it was through them, deeply and intimately, that Jesus Christ was announced, conceived and heralded (Luke, 1 and 2). They entered deeply into the life and work of Jesus, coming to support his human weakness and brokenness in Gethsemane (Luke 22.43). These presences do not disappear in the light of the Resurrection, but rather herald and, as it were, orchestrate it, thus linking it with the Nativity; again they manifest themselves after the Ascension, and announce the coming of the Holy Spirit (Acts 1.10). Finally, it is clear that these spirits have a central presence and role in what is called the 'salvation of souls', rejoicing in the conversion of the sinner (Luke 15.7), assisting at and orchestrating the Final Judgment (Matt. 25.31). In one of the most unexpected and characteristic of those *Logia* or sayings attributed to Jesus Christ Himself, it is clearly implied that every human person has an angel or angels overlighting their earthly journey. Speaking of what are called the 'little ones' — and this may well include the childlike as well as children — He says: 'Be careful that you do not despise any one of these little ones, for their angels in heaven have at all times the vision of my Father Who is in the heavens' (Matt. 18.10). The implication here is that every man, woman and child has an angel in the heavens, and this belief is also assumed in the story of Peter's release from prison in *Acts*: not only is this accomplished through an angel but when his companions are told that he is at the door they say 'it must be his angel' (Acts 12.15. The NEB translates: 'it must be his guardian angel').

The angels come and go along the track of the various New Testament narratives, and this presence extends to the early Christian community living in the memory of Jesus of Nazareth and the glow of the Risen Christ. But when we look deeper we find that this messenger role of the good spirits is but the external manifestation of their continual and substantial presence in that very region or sphere towards which every word and every event is directed, that is to say the Kingdom of Heaven, or 'the heavens'. This is the region from which Jesus had come, and to which he returns, as he ascends into 'the clouds', which act as the curtains of this kingdom, for all through the New Testament (as also in the Old Testament) the physical sky and its phenomena act as the interface between the visible world or *cosmos* and the invisible world or *ouranos*. The contemporaries of the New Testament writers understand this, having still a sense of 'the mountain behind the mountain', as of the world within the world, that could in heightened perception become manifest.

Now this invisible world was not only the world of the Father, Son and Holy Spirit but also the world of the angels. So it is that the definitive Christian prayer, what we name the Lord's Prayer, is full of the angelic presences, for we pray to 'Our Father who is in the heavens', and we ask that all things on earth should become filled with the atmosphere of the heavens, which is the vibrancy and power of the Divine Will. Notice that the Greek original of this prayer does not have the singular, 'heaven', as in the English translation but rather 'heavens' as in the Latin, French and German versions: the singular might indeed seem to focus only on the deity, but the plural clearly affirms the variety and multitude of the angelic hosts and hierarchies. If 'the heavens' is the Father's house of many mansions, and the homeland of all our deepest yearnings, it is also the region of total companionship, where our guardian spirits are leading us and await us in the company of the faithful departed, the dead who are most of all alive in *terra viventium,* the land of the living and of true life.

Now what Celtic Christianity has always clearly realised is that this other world is very near to us, and in a sense perceptible to the Christian imagination. It is a Christian consciousness in living continuity with the pagan consciousness which peopled valleys, mountains, rivers, lakes, islands and woodland with presences invisible but not entirely incorporeal, alien yet essentially open to human communication. Clearly this visionary world had its darknesses and extravagances, yet it provided the space and ambience within which the spirit-world of the Christian revelation could be fully and practically accommodated. This glory of God's holy angels, this region of heavenly involvement with the earth and its problems and miseries, is still available to us today as readers and hearers of the Word of God in Christ. But we need to open to it fully and deeply; we need to receive it in freedom, for it will not, cannot, force an entry into our world.

B But even if it be admitted that angels come and go constantly in the pages of the New Testament, and even if it be further admitted that to look deeper is to find them more deeply present, the contemporary Christian or 'seeker' may ask why they are important to us now and in the days ahead. Why must one look to them in shaping a new design for Christian and cosmic living? Is not Christ sufficient, indeed more than sufficient, to reshape all damaged beauty to a new splendour? Does not St. Paul warn us that any undue magnifying of the angels is a return to paganism, and a total failure to grasp the meaning of the Cross and the Resurrection of the one Saviour and Mediator (Col. 2.18)? Is not the Son of Man exalted above all the angelic hierarchies, whence he calls us to eternal fellowship as Sons of God?

This view, though it obviously contains much of what is called Christian doctrine, is nonetheless based on a total misunderstanding of God, of Christ, of man and of creation. It is a misunderstanding of God, because it presents us with a lonely deity in an empty heavens overhanging a material cosmos of empty space and monotonous time. It is no wonder that this far-off and inaccessible God has succumbed in man's imagination to the huge desolation and emptiness that surrounds him. This God is indeed dead, and we cannot bring him back to life, or if he lives we cannot any longer ascend to him in the fiery chariots of Biblical imagination. It is a misunderstanding of Christ, for on the one hand his terrifying and agonising descent into the world of the Fallen Angels (even into Hell and the region of everlasting death) becomes meaningless, and on the other his elevation as the Son of Man (and of the Woman) above all the angelic hierarchies becomes mere rhetoric, and loses its 'clouds of glory', all its ambience in the *sanctus* of the angelic liturgy. It is a misunderstanding of man, because manwomanhood is no longer the bridge between the two orders of creation, spirit and matter, but is only a peak of lonely and absurd intellectuality emerging above the vast chaos of the universe in one small corner of it. All man's spirit companions have departed, and he is left alone in the face of a lonely God: man the mediator is dead. It is a misunderstanding of Creation, because not only is the material earth an affront to the purity and eternal radiance of the Most High God (and therefore totally expendable and closed to transformation), but the material heavens with its millions of galaxies has lost all its meaning as the interface of the invisible hierarchies. We do not, we cannot, realise that space-travel is not primarily a physical journey, but a deepening and clarifying of our perception beyond and sometimes away from the universe revealed by our telescopes. Dante's 'love that moves the sun and the other stars' has lost its seraphic presence and splendour.

We do not have to find a context for the world of these spirits within our theology and cosmology. *Au contraire,* it is the spirit-world that completes our theology and gives context to our cosmology.

So it is that the cosmic vision of Celtic Christianity is not only continuous with the cosmic vision of the New Testament, but is the only vision large and deep enough to provide a complete and satisfying account of Creation and Redemption. If we are to have a new design for Christian self-understanding we must recover this vision.

C When we come to ask how we can recover this vision of a cosmos peopled by angels as well as men and women, and all that lives and moves and vibrates all around us, we must first of all realise that what we are doing is affirming a tradition that has in fact never quite disappeared from Christian theology, at least in its Catholic and Orthodox manifestations, a tradition which, as we have just seen, has its living source in the New Testament. It is often forgotten, even by those who know him as *Doctor Angelicus,* that St. Thomas Aquinas, the theologian who dominated Catholic theology and philosophy up to quite recently, and is indeed returning again, was so called because of the central place he accorded to the angelic world in his theology. The Hellenistic philosophy, which in its Aristotelian form he accepted so fully and developed so marvellously, gave him the thought-world, the horizon or dimensions, for this, but only because this mighty firmament of spirit-being could be seen clearly reflected in the deep waters of the Christian Revelation. Our new design cannot be simply a revival of Thomism, for this was in many ways severely marked by the limitations of the medieval mind, which for instance could only see the non-Christian world as marginal, and made the mistake of thinking that Christianity was a doctrine already fully understood, and that in one way only. But it can look to this mighty vision for guidance, and for a sense of continuity.

St. Thomas' treatise on 'spiritual creatures which Holy Scripture calls angels' occupies a central place in the First Part of the *Summa Theologiae*, and runs to fourteen questions: in the standard Dominican Edition, which includes text, translation and notes, it is a stout volume of over 300 pages.[34] It is a philosophical and theological work of marvellous depth, range and subtlety, and it is with this treatise that any attempt to recover the ancient metaphysics of spiritual substance must begin. At first sight some of the topics raised in these seventy or more *articuli* will perhaps seem over-subtle, and may indeed recall the humanistic gibe about angels dancing on a needle. Neither Thomas nor any of the medieval theologians raised this question, and if it had been raised Thomas would have brushed it aside by saying that since angels were free of all materiality the question did not arise. Yet, curiously, a very important point has arisen here, one in which Thomas went

---

[34] St Thomas Aquinas, *Summa Theologiae*, Eyre and Spottiswoode, London, Vol. 9.

against most of the tradition. For he, almost alone among the great scholastics, said that angels are totally immaterial, pure spirit without admixture of any kind of matter, even matter of a special celestial or 'spiritual' kind. This left him with the problem of how angels could become visible at times, and could otherwise intervene in the material world. It would be interesting to compare Thomas' doctrine here with that of Duns Scotus, who came out of the Celtic world — indeed from a little place not far from where I am writing this, in Edinburgh, Scotland. Scotus argued for several physical regions, several levels of materiality, and I feel that this allows more room both for the biblical data and for the kind of everyday presences of angels that we find in the Celtic folk-tradition of, say, the *Carmina Gadelica*.

Clearly there is much scholarly and creative work to be done if we are to bring the medieval metaphysical theology of angels into such close relationship with the continuous Celtic folk tradition that they begin to form a single design centering and enriching the wider design of a complete theology enclosing a total cosmology.

This creative fusion of high philosophical speculation with the colourful and deeply woven Christian praxis of the oldest folk-culture of the West is surely an attractive proposal, and one in any case worth any while we can devote to it. But all the same, it will not do as it stands. It does not provide us with a new design that takes full account of the present in order to help us fashion the future. It does not face the fact of science, the fact of technology, the fact of urbanisation. It does not provide a cosmic imagination to enclose the world of nuclear physics, the explorations of space, genetic manipulation, and the rest. It can only withdraw before the Great Dragon who is now so enormously menacing. We must, so to speak, find a place for the Dragon within the tapestry of our design, and for this we must return to Teilhard, bringing with us that which has remained outside or outwith his cosmology: the angelic world in all its presence and possibilities.

III. Cosmogenesis and Cosmic Persons

It must be said firmly at this point that, apart from Teilhard, there is nobody else. There are many theologians who are scientists and/or philosophers, but there is nobody who brings science and theology together in a philosophical synthesis that not only finds room for both but has both working fully together in one harness. None of Teilhard's critics achieve this, or even attempt to achieve it, any more than did any of the critics of Christopher Columbus explore the far reaches of the Atlantic, or even attempt to do so. And as Columbus was the herald of a New World very different from that which he envisaged, so too Teilhard is perhaps opening our imaginations to a new design far different from anything he was able to see.

What Teilhard's vision provides is a grandiose unification of what he names the three infinities which science has discovered: the infinitely great, the infinitely small, and the infinitely complex. This he does by the two polar concepts of radial energy and Christogenesis, with the linking concepts of Omega, complexity-consciousness and Cosmogenesis, and the governing principle: union differentiates. In this vast enterprise of unification, his evidence, the materials with which he works, his paint-box so to speak, has two sources: what are called the findings of science, on the one hand, and the Christology of St. Paul and St. John, on the other. In this vision the radial energy that flows through the whole universe is seen as continuous with the radiance of the Risen Christ in the glory of the Trinity.

Now Teilhard did not anywhere in his writings refer to the Catholic theology of the angels, which he would have absorbed from his strongly devotional family ambience. He turned his eyes and his mind resolutely in the direction of matter, and steadfastly refused to allow any doctrine of a spirit-world to obscure this concern with matter in its inviolable materiality. Yet it was this hardheaded exploration of matter that brought him to the 'imagination' of radial energy, which is in fact a threshold concept uniting matter and spirit, or rather focusing the spirit-element at the root of the matter. For spirit is the being that mirrors being, each and every being that surrounds it, and finally in its deepest spirit-reality mirrors itself precisely as mirrored being. And the opening of spirit-being to all being and the All-Being, or Omega, is precisely the primary movement of Love, the Hospitality of Being in the midst of being, the ultimate Home-Light of the Father's House reflected in every monad of creation. So it is that Teilhard can say that, unless this light of love is somehow present in the basic elements of the universe, it would not be present in man and woman at the highest level we know.

Now when Teilhard speaks of radial energy, and the basic monads as centres of love and primitive consciousness, he is telling us that the universe is everywhere a personal and personalising plenum. Everywhere, from its earliest beginnings. But in this plenum all meaning centres on the human, which as we know does not emerge for millions of years, and then comes to inhabit just one small corner of the universe. So we have a universe full of personal meaning, instinct with personality, yet without the living presence of any fully realised persons: all these are in the making, waiting for the breakthrough of 'hominisation' and the emergence of the 'noosphere'. But this is a personalising universe in which there are no persons to shape and guide it. Yes, there is the Creator, of course, and it can be argued that the 'divine milieu' is active at all points of space and time. Yet there is in this cosmology a great void between the Creator and the basic monads of his creation, which is strictly inconceivable. To put it pictorially: God cannot create a void in order to create a cosmos beyond the void. The supremely personal being can only work his works by way of persons. In other words, the personalising or pre-personal universe of Teilhard can have meaning only within a universe of cosmic persons. More concretely, the angels must be seen to be there from the first beginnings of the physical universe. This is one of the central insights of another cosmic thinker, a younger contemporary of Teilhard, Charles Winckelmans de Cléty, whose book, *The World of Persons*, appeared in 1967 with forewards from two distinguished philosophers, but which nonetheless aroused little or no interest. The academic world was not yet ready to talk about cosmic persons.[35]

The illimitable cosmos of stars and galaxies is cold, lonely and meaningless, unless we see it as the setting of a multitude of 'cosmic persons' shimmering through the veils of perception, and lighting the candles of imagination. But it is only if we find these spirits in the ordinary and everyday, as does the Celtic religious imagination, that we can look up and feel their bright and benevolent presence in the circling stars and the receding galaxies. In our own time, in my own lifetime, astronomy has extended the human cosmic imagination until it has snapped: we must recover at all costs the homeliness and awesome grandeur (as of a royal inheritance) of the physical heavens. Teilhard alone has given us back the grandeur of this heritage; only the Christian angels in their Celtic immediacy can restore its homeliness.

The other pole of Teilhard's Cosmogenesis is Christogenesis, which has recovered for our day a cosmic Christology that goes back to Origen, and is firmly rooted in St. John and St. Paul.[36] Christ is the Word who is from the beginning, and through whom all things are made, all things down to the last blade of

---

[35] *The World of Persons*. Burns and Oates, 1967.
[36] See Lyons *op. cit.*, ch. 1.

grass and the least speck of dust (John 1.8). In him all things are held together; in the end he takes all things unto himself to subject them to the Father, so that God may be all in all (Col. 1.17;1 Cor.15.8). But this conception, which is true to the New Testament text as far as it goes, nevertheless omits or overlooks that whole great hierarchical vision by which, for Paul especially, Jesus Christ is given his proper and crowning place and glory in the great harmony of creation. Indeed this is precisely the meaning, in its context, of the text from Colossians (1.17) that Teilhard is so fond of quoting, for what is held together by him is firstly the world of the cosmic powers 'the invisible orders of thrones, sovereignties, authorities and powers' (1.17 NEB), that is to say the traditional 'choirs of angels', or hierarchies. By omitting this central aspect of the original cosmic vision Teilhard puts a heavy strain on what MacDonald calls our intellecto-imaginative faculty of visualisation, as we look out at the earth and sea and sky, and seek the physical presence of the Incarnate Logos in every particle and monad. He is there, yes (as *she*, Mary, is too, in a sense as Queen of Angels) but his presence is a centering of a thousand million spiritual presences each with its place and function in the mighty harmony of the heavens and the earth.

St. Paul names 'the authorities and powers' in another place, where he tells us that our fight is not against human foes, but against Cosmic Powers, 'against the authorities and potentates of this dark world, against the superhuman forces of evil in the heavens' (Ephes. 6.10). It is because of the reality of the evil spirits, the Fallen Angels, that such a large part of the Celtic domestic and pastoral liturgy was protective and invocational. Teilhard must have been conscious of this kind of prayer in the Divine Office which he dutifully recited every day, and in the Eucharistic Liturgy which likewise he celebrated daily. Yet he did not find a place for the cosmic powers of destruction in his cosmic vision. He had to do what he had to do, already an enormous task, and this in his time and place, as a scientist in dialogue with scientists, did not allow any kind of steady gaze at the world of cosmic spirits. It is for us to fill in the bright colours, and to find a place for the dark ones.

Most of all, it is for us to recover the Celtic tradition of protective and liberating invocation, which is deeply rooted in the New Testament and the Old, and has its echoes in almost all religious traditions. For although we are in a world of God's beneficent power and purposes, and in the epoch of Christ's victory over Satan, nevertheless we are in a world of freedom, that ambiguous and vulnerable human freedom that can so easily connive with the Powers of Evil. There is a sense in which our political and public world is held prisoner by these forces, and of course we are part of that thraldom. How can we break it, for ourselves and for the World? How can we delineate and establish a new design as we look over the century's end and into the third Christian millennium?

IV. A Fusion of Horizons

From every point of view the question of our planetary future is a question of energy, of physical energy in all its levels and varieties, of spirit energy in all *its* levels and varieties. All that has emerged so far in this study adds up to an affirmation of the unity in continuity of these two energies. Already this unity is assumed in all Christian liturgies: prayer works wonders, works what are called miracles, which simply means that there are open lines of causality between the two worlds. Not the breaking of natural laws, but the linking of two realms of natural law by way of human freedom. In our Western technical civilisation this link has been broken: only the Celtic consciousness has preserved the freedom to continue it, largely because it has become marginalised as a folk-culture. To it we must go to forge anew this link between physical energy and spirit-energy.

Here the angels are our friends and fellow citizens. It is generally overlooked how central a role the angels have had in Christian worship from the beginning. The congregation we see is overlighted by the heavenly congregation we do not see, so much so that St. Paul uses their accepted presence, fairly or unfairly, to support his ideas on feminine decorum (I Cor. 11.10). In the traditional Latin mass (now partly surviving as the first Eucharistic Prayer) the angels are invoked not only to pray that we be forgiven our sins (at the *Confiteor*) but also to accompany the congregation in the most solemn prayer or glory, the Sanctus or *Trisagion*, and to take the offered sacrifice to God's altar in heaven, seen as the heavenly counterpart of the earthly altar. All this is within the context of the glorified Christ, who is Lord and King, and also of the totally human Virgin Mary who is invoked as *Regina Angelorum*, Queen of the Angels.

Much more could be said about this world of spirit-energy and its intimate relationship with physical or material energy, but I want to bring in a third energy which is in fact nearer to Teilhard's radial energy than is either of the other two. This is love-energy, that which for Dante 'moves the sun and the other stars', as it also binds together all human loves and lovers. Teilhard has pointed to the fact that only a very small part of this energy is needed for human procreation, and it has moreover come to be seen in our time that homosexual *eros* cannot simply be outlawed as unnatural and perverse: it is simply a fact of nature that has to be taken seriously and with respect. This was how Plato saw it, and this, if we are to take the sonnets in their plain meaning, is how Shakespeare saw it. Not rejection but transcendence, not the 'waste of shame' but Socratic chastity, not self-indulgence but austerity, not that possessiveness in which the gaoler becomes also the prisoner and the prisoner the gaoler, but that high and holy freedom of noble companionship and mystical tenderness. For most people, however, *eros* in its maturer presence is the energy that unites feminine and masculine in all its varieties of pain and joy, of glory and shame, of understanding and misunderstanding. For the Christian tradition it has its proper fulfilment in marriage and family, which for St. Paul, as for St. Thomas later on, is the living sign and *locus* of the union of Christ and the Church. But when all is said, this more ordinary and natural *eros* poses the very same challenge of transcendence and liberation as does homosexual *eros*. Nowhere on the face of the planet, not even within the most sacred precincts of the most stable family, can there be possessive love between two people without bondage and destructiveness. In all cases *eros* must be liberated; in all cases it is a 'divine' energy in the sense that it has unlimited aspirations, and it must be given the freedom of its holy source, if human beings are to be happy in themselves, and free to build a new earth together. This was the vision of celibacy — not isolation as in later distortions of it, but men and women working closely together for a common ideal — which activated the early Christians, as is clear from a careful reading of *First Corinthians*. Without the rediscovery of celibacy, and of Christian marriage *within* it, there cannot be a new design to reshape the ravaged beauty of Christendom. For love-energy is the only energy we have that is more powerful than aggressiveness and 'that acquisitiveness which is an idolatry'.

It must be admitted that the liberation of this energy may come only in the wake of destroying angels of apocalyptic power and terror.

But this too can be seen positively. I can cooperate with both the cleansing and clearing processes of the 'destroying' angel, and from there go on to work with the higher power that helps me to rebuild my own world and the world around me. This is where the spirit-energy re-enters as the energy of prayer, that which formed the substance of the hidden life of Jesus, and in which the angels supported him when he most needed support. The energy of prayer is at once of earth and of the heavens. It is the meeting point of man and woman with the Father in 'the heavens'. it is a sharing in the heavenly liturgy which vibrates in the background of the New Testament, and comes into clear manifestation at the Nativity and the Resurrection, as also in *Revelation*. In the ancient *Prefaces* of the Mass we are open fully and frankly to this heavenly liturgy. *Et ideo cum angelis et archangelis. So with the Angels and the Archangels, with the Thrones and Dominations, with the whole host of the heavenly army we sing a hymn of Thy glory.* And in some of these *Prefaces* we pray after the invocation of the heavenly host 'that our voices should blend with theirs'. These are strong words spoken with full deliberation as the People of God address themselves to the living centre of their most solemn common act of worship. Surely this energy of prayer that moves into this other world returns augmented and transformed, and holds the possibility of the transformation of love-energy in a new miracle of unification.

It was a principle in some of the 'Mystery Religions' that opened the way for the coming of Christ that the only way to defeat the Dragon is 'to enter the skin of the Dragon'. This does not mean becoming like the Dragon, or even taking on the shape of the Dragon, but rather entering into the place or lair of the Dragon. That is what Jesus Christ did in Gethsemane when 'horror and dismay came over him' (Mark 14.34), and he prayed to the Father to spare him from this hour: this prayer announces the Passion and Death of Jesus in all four Gospels, announces that entry into the place of Satan, the *hypogeum* of unending death, the Darkness Itself. He survived and triumphed, and rose again, and ascended to the Father. From where he is 'in the heavens', with the Cosmic Powers of Light beneath him and the Dragon defeated, from there, far-off and near, he calls us towards him, calls us to come after him along that same road that he has travelled, by way of Gethsemane and Calvary. For the Dragon is not slain but only defeated or brought into captivity.

It seems to me that two things above all else have been accomplished by the love-energy and prayer-energy of the Word made flesh: first the mighty flowing forth, like a river or a great storm, of the Spirit of God through the glorified manhood of the ascended Son of Mary, flowing through all the hierarchies into the human world and the world of nature: second, the gradual conquest and utilisation of the lost energies of the Fallen Angels, as these cosmic persons are painfully brought back into the universal harmony. The early Christians lived in the radiance of the first of these consequences of the Death and Resurrection of Christ, and seeing only this with everyday clarity, they did not see the long road ahead for the Church and the world, though this was implied and hinted at in the New Testament itself. At the end of two thousand years in which the hidden energies of the earth have been discovered and exploited, at the end of which the Dragon has come to confront us in the full beauty and terror of his power, we can see clearly how real and challenging is this second consequence of the mighty deeds of Christ. As the first Christians turned away from the world (the *cosmos* for which Jesus did *not* pray: John 17), so we latter-day Christians are greatly tempted to turn away from this newly discovered world of nuclear energy, and with it all that comes under the head of advanced technology, and what it offers in the way of shaping our planetary future. And we have no lack of Prophets of Doom who tell us that the end is near.

In the face of all this we need a strong affirmation of our human, earthly future, and it is my contention that the time has come for the Christian Commonwealth — to use T. S. Eliot's terminology — to recover its kinship with those cosmic persons that are called 'angels' in the New Testament and the

Christian tradition, and whose everyday presence and radiance is still with us in the remnants of Celtic Christianity.

But this vision alone cannot enclose the world of science and technology, cannot present us with an 'imagination' close enough to scientific theory and observation to provide a new design that can take into itself the shape of the world we inhabit. Teilhard, and Teilhard alone, provides this, in his vision of a universe of radial energy reaching towards total 'amorisation' and personalisation in the Cosmic Christ. And it is Teilhard himself who tells us that if his vision is true it will be transcended in a larger vision, for such is the way of cosmogenesis.

Yet it would be dangerous, as we fashion our new design, to move very far away from the world of George MacDonald, the world of those stories written 'for children of all ages'. A design must never become a military-style plan of campaign, and there are passages in Teilhard where this all-too-disastrously happens. It must not lose its lightness and mystery, its holiness as of a prayer ever renewing itself. For indeed the Lord's Prayer is essentially the 'new design' of the Christian Commonwealth 'on earth as it is in heaven'. And the angel who stands guard over a new world in the making surely reflects the beauty of the all-fathering, all-mothering God, and the home-light of that place 'where glory dwells'.

10

MEMORY AND THE IMAGINAL WORLD: THE 'KEENING' TRADITION

I

What an elegaic poem or song of remembrance does is to bring the dead past to life. But it might seem that this life, this vividness of recall is negatived and indeed mocked by the hard factuality of the pastness of the past and the pathos arising from the memory of the days that are no more. 'They are all gone, the old familiar faces.' Charles Lamb who wrote this line is almost the prophet of this vanishing of the past. But does the past really vanish? Does it vanish without trace? Is not the elegy itself, the threnody itself, the Gaelic 'keening' literature in all its width and depth, in all its creative urgency and permanence — is all this merely a trace, and no more than a trace, of what has passed away? Does the light of memory, 'the light of other days', in Thomas Moore's phrase, shine on a world of ghosts, or does it not rather shine on the eternal as it was and is present within what *seems* (to our seeming selves) to have passed away? If there is an 'imaginal' or 'subtle' world present and sometimes sensed even by our gross corruptible senses in their more 'spiritual' moments — if this is so in any real sense then is it not possible that this eternal or ethereal world shines most clearly within the depths of the waters of memory?[37]

---

[37] The concept of the imaginal world will be found under various terminologies in some well-known writers such as C. J. Jung (*Memories, Dreams and Reflections*), Rudolf Steiner (*Occult Science*) and Mircea Eiade

Let us look at this horizon from the standpoint of the Christian 'revelation' as set down in the New Testament. Let us look at that strange ritual in which Jesus took bread and wine and blessed them both and shared them out among his disciples and said: '*This is my body; this is the chalice of my blood; take, and drink*' (Luke 22.17). Then he adds: *do this in memory of me*. It seems that here we are in the presence of a kind of presence that cuts across the stream of time. This is already hinted at by the reference to the Crucifixion, which is in the future, yet is also in the past and in the present (which *is given* for you: *to didomenon*) as if the event of the Crucifixion in its total and essential meaning broke through time and its radiance shone backwards to the beginning and onwards to the end. It must be recalled that the bread and wine ritual made present, by way of the hymns that were said, all the great events in the history of the chosen people of God. It is as if Jesus made everything present in becoming totally present as the sacrificial lamb of God and as if the hymns of remembrance became hymns of presence.

All human life passes away, passes very swiftly away, yet the very poems and songs which express this evanescence of all things human do in a real sense escape from this evanescence.

(*Myths, Dreams and Mysteries*). Outstanding among those who deal with the concept directly is the French writer on Sufi mysticism, Henry Corbin (*Spiritual Body and Celestial Earth*, Bollinger Series XCI, Princeton UP 1977); the Scottish writer Robert Crookall (*Ecstasy: The Release of the Soul from the Body*, Mornabad, India 1973); The Jungian or Post-Jungian American writer of Latvian origin, Roberts Avens (*Imaginal Body*, University Press of America 1982); G. R. S. Mead (*The Doctrine of the Subtle Body in Western Tradition* London: Stuart and Watkins 1967).

But perhaps the most powerful testimony to the imaginal world is that given by a magazine called *Temenos* first published in 1981 under the editorship (mainly) of Kathleen Raine. See especially Temenos I, now out of print, but available in some libraries. Temenos 8 which has a remarkable article by Henry Corbin is still available through Element books, Shaftesbury, Dorset SP7 8PL.

The poem or song eternalises the instant, and the more it shows forth the beauties of form and harmony the more truly and fully it does this, bringing with it something of the peace of eternity. So it is that there is a close connection between the Celtic folk-imagination that opened to the various realms of the imaginal world, the other world of the *leannaun shee* and *tir-na-nog* and 'the good dead in the green hills' — there is a real connexion between all this and the elegaic tradition of the *caoine* or 'keening' poetry and song, and the 'keening' women of the traditional Irish 'wake', the wake immortalised by James Joyce in his almost inaccessible phantasmagoria *Finnegan's Wake*, wherein everything comes round again like the waters of the Liffey that flows into the first lines of the book and flows out again at the end, which thus becomes the beginning.

Friedrich Nietzsche, we know, played around with the notion of eternal recurrence, but neither Nietzsche nor Joyce possessed the key without which all doctrines of eternal recurrence get lost in the wastes of their historical factuality and materiality, or in the triviality of *deja vu* parapsychology. What 'recurs' is not the material event but the inner 'spirit' or meaning of the material event as revealed, say, in the 'Proustian moment' of illumination from within which a whole world can be recreated.[38]

[38] The most directly autobiographical account of these moments of involuntary recall of 'lost' time is to be found in the *Preface* to Proust's *Contre Saint-Beuve* (paris, Gallimand, 1954), and of course they are woven fictionally into the narrator's story in *A la Recherche de Temps Perdu*. As related in the *Preface* to *Contre Saint Beuve* Proust returning chilled to his rooms is given a cup of tea and some fingers of toast by his old housekeeper, dips the toast in the tea and tastes it. That very simple taste sensation opens up a whole past world to him as it connects with a similar sensation of toast or biscuit dipped in tea from the far past, a sensation long forgotten or 'lost' with the 'lostness' of the past. It is especially because he attended carefully to this kind of moment that Proust could write his great novel wherein a

This recreation is a work of memory, yet the light by which it is recreated is not that which shone, fleetingly and moment by moment, within the past and is now vanished *with* the past. It is another light as of another world that emerges from within the past through the work of imagination. It is in a sense the light of imagination revealing another world, other than that which arises through a mere recall of the past. There is within the past a light that somehow connects ordinary time with another dimension of time, the dimension that opens up at what T. S. Eliot calls 'the point of intersection of the timeless with time'. At that point of intersection the past events which have been taken away by time are somehow found again and show forth a new significance and indeed generate a special feeling that is not really a sadness for what has gone forever but a kind of joy or release in the realisation that there is a sense in which our past experiences, and those of others, still retain their connexion with the source, and that a light from the source somehow shines through the vanishings of the past. All through his *Four Quarters* T. S. Eliot strives towards this light by means of all the resources of his poetic or 'making' art.[39] For dark and broken world becomes luminous and 'heavenly' through the art of a writer of genius. Mary Warnock in her book on *Memory* (Faber and Faber, 1987) stresses the connexion of Proust with Chateuabriand and quotes from the latter a passage which illustrates the connexion between music and that memory which cuts across time. Mary Warnock writes as follows (p. 98): 'Chateuabriand was aware both of the power and also of the essential privacy of memory. Writing about his childhood home of Combourg, he said: 'If after reading this somewhat lengthy description, an artist took up his pencil could he produce a good likeness of the Chateau? I doubt it ... Such is the impotence of words and the power of memory to evoke material things. In beginning to speak of Combourg, I am singing the first couplets of a lament that will have charms for no one but myself (*Memories of Childhood and Youth*, Ms of 1826).'

[39] See Morris Weitz: *T. S. Eliot: Time as a mode of salvation* in T. S. Eliot: *Four Quarters: Critical Essays* edited by B. Bergonzi, Macmillan Press 1969).

Eliot it is only by connexion with the Christian God that the events of time have meaning, otherwise time is simply 'a ridiculous waste stretching before and after'. Yet it is by the poets' art rather than by way of faith that this presence of an emergent transcendence within time is sought and found.

II

The voice and voices of remembrance by which the vanished past reappears in the present are central to the Celtic folk-tradition in its various forms. Indeed there were in parts of Ireland until quite recently 'keening women' who had special vocal and imaginative skills in expressing grief for the dead and bringing the dead present to the common consciousness of the community by way of memory and imagination.

Perhaps the purest example of this class of keening-poetry that has survived is that composed by Eileen Dubh Ni Conaill on the sudden death of her husband Art O'Leary. (Notice that in the Irish and also the Scottish Gaelic tradition up to our own day a woman kept her own family name after marriage.) In her sorrow and in order to express it this woman picks, quite naturally and without hesitation (for so the keening-song came forth), clear sharp images out of her memory so that out of the rhythm and imaginative clarity of the poem and the clear melodious voices of the keening-woman a radiance of beauty arises, linking unconsciously but naturally this drop of beauty with the great ocean of that original beauty that is one of the aspects of the Source of all life and all creation, the Lord of life and death.

> Strong was our love
> From the day that I saw you
> By the market-house gable.
> All eye was I seeing you
> All heart was our meeting...

It rises within me,
That fine day in Spring
That gleam of gold braid
On your hat-band: the silver
Sheen of sword-handle
And the brave hand that held it
Fearless and fearful
To every dark enemy[40]

The sad beauty of the woman's keening-song — its vivid images and plangent harmonies of sound, emerges as life within death, as the delicate presence of beauty showing itself by way of that human imagination in which the past is connected with the hidden source of all human love and endeavour. It is in the departure, for ever, of her 'half-bed companion' and the depths of great grief that imagination awakens in these words and images that have shone across the centuries.

The relief of sorrow that comes through the expression of sorrow by way of imagination is already at hand in ritual, or newly minted, as in the case of Eileen Dubh. There is a stirring of life, however muted, within the grief which, as modern psychology has discovered, decompresses the deathly power of the loss and affirms life. There is always a connexion, however tenuous, between the absence that is death and the presence that is human feeling and the community of mourning. This touches not only the people who have gone but also the times that have gone. Through the popular songs of remembrance such as *Auld Lang Syne*, that which has passed away is brought

---

[40]See O. Tuama and Kinsella, *Poems of the Dispossessed 1600–1900* (Mountrath, Ireland. The Dolmen Press, 1981, pp. 200ff.). This book gives the Irish-Gaelic text with English translations. The translation here is by the present writer and is more 'free' than that of Thomas Kinsella.

present to each of us and socialised, and indeed eternalised, taken outside of time by way of memory and imagination. A lost world is found by being looked at in the eternal light of memory and imagination, eternal because it comes ultimately from the source of our being which in the neoplatonic Augustinian strand of the Great Tradition touches our minds directly as an inner illumination. All songs and poems of remembrance are reflections of this light and lead back to it.

III

Eileen Dubh's keening song expressing a personal grief within a family and neighbourly community comes from the later part of the eighteenth century, that terrible century of dispossession in which the shameful cruel, rapacious side of England was turned towards Ireland to possess its land and enslave its people. Let us not put the blame on England, the land of the muses, but rather on that obscene and satanic force in all nations and peoples which exploits and oppresses the poor and the weak. Let us remember, also, that a succession of people of English Protestant descent from Wolfe Tone to Maude Gonne gave their strength and their lives to bring some measure of freedom to Ireland.

This was two centuries on from that terrible eighteenth century in which the Irish Jacobite poets wrote some of the most moving lamentations for a broken and ravaged nation that have ever been written. Outstanding among those was Aogan O'Rahilly (1675–1729) whose greatest poems are 'aislings' or imaginary visions of a beautiful woman (Eire or Ireland) who waits longingly for her true prince (the Stuart Pretender) but who is held captive and dishonoured by a cruel, powerful loutish John Bull (Shaun O Dee as he was sometimes called). Within this framework O'Rahilly wrote some exquisite poetry of lamentation for the old Gaelic order that was passing away and thus gave a whole oppressed people words and images that radiated something of eternal beauty. This beauty established itself by the very power of imagination as having its own indestructible reality, a reality not created but discovered by the art of the poet.

O'Rahilly's greatest poem 'Brightness of Brightness' resists translation. However Thomas Kinsella himself a poet of distinction has done his best, and the first stanza in this version reads as follows:

> Brightness most bright I beheld on the way, forlorn
> Crystal of crystal her eye, blue touched with green,
> Sweetness most sweet her voice, not stern with age
> Colour and pallor appeared on her flushed cheeks[41]

This is painfully literal: the words are all there shivering, naked, in cold English, and yet every single touch of the magic has gone. How can one convey O'Rahilly's image? In the first place *Gile na gile,* though it is sufficiently translated as 'Brightness most bright', can also, even more literally be rendered 'brightness of brightness' which indicates that first pull upwards of the vision into another sphere, a sphere of essences, of that inner beauty and radiance which Hopkins calls 'inscape' and Hans Urs von Balthasar the 'form' of beauty after the analogy of the Aristotelian form as the 'soul' or life-principle in all living things. The 'brightness' of brightness is not simply 'great' brightness or 'most bright' brightness or even 'dazzling' brightness (though this is somewhat better). Rather is there question

---

[41]See *Poems of the Dispossessed* p. 150, 151. It should be noted that the imaginal world for all its 'thereness' allows for the freedom of an imagination not *bound* by perception. This means that a poet translating a poet will, *as* a poet, tend to produce his own poem. Thomas Kinsella seems conscious of this and does not translate *as* a poet but rather as a translator whom the common reader can trust at his level. This is fine in its way, yet the reader sometimes senses the frustration of the poet who is unable to emerge.

of a liminal or boundary experience in which another world shines through, physical but not of the order of the everyday corruptible physical, a physical form without that physical matter which is restless and seeking other forms to invest it, but rather form investing a heavenly matter, the *Materia Coelestis* of the Ancients. All through the poem this imaginal quality belongs to the heavenly woman or *speirbhean* and it stands contrasted with the world of coarse goblins and their cyclopean master who hold the woman prisoner. The poem ends in lamentation and exclamations of sorrow piled one on the other, with just a faint glimmer of hope that 'the lions may come over the sea'.

But the power and reality of the poem does not rest on the hope but rather on the presence of beauty not only in the vision of the sky-woman but in the art by which the whole experience is presented, and what this art reveals within and beyond itself, the 'more-than beautiful' of Plotinus that has been made present within the beauty of the vision by means of the poet's art. Within the dark distress of eighteenth-century Ireland a light appears (one among many) that is Wordsworth's 'light that never was on sea and land'. The ancient world is passing away, yet still the poet holds it in memory as Eileen Dubh held her man in memory, and through the power of poetic imagination, that memory and those memories are seen in the *memoria Dei* in which all is gathered in through what Yeats calls 'the artifice of eternity'.

IV

In all this it becomes clear that poetry, music and song bring up the half remembered images of the past, the near past or the far past, and take these images into another sphere. The images within the memory, what could be set down as historical 'fact', are, as it were, dressed in rags and tatters. What poetic imagination does is take some of these images and, by way of magic indeed, dress them in the clothes of another world and in the light of eternal beauty. It is in this process that something of the eternal beauty and truth that radiates from and through the past is revealed. Partly created, yet not only created but discovered as well. To mourn the past is not simply to feel and express the pain of its passing away. it is rather to call up its inner, eternal meaning and substance by bringing to bear on it the light of beauty which is in its depths one with the light of being, of unity, of truth, of goodness.

If then we are to retrieve the past in its eternality, in its deepest meaning, we have to bring to bear on it the light of beauty through the medium of art, all the way from the voice of prayer to the voice of the keening woman who stands at the threshold of life and death as rightfully as does the priest.

It is Plato who first noticed the deep connexion between beauty and timelessness and between the desire for beauty and the desire for creation at various levels, ultimately a desire for immortality. (Symposium 207ff). That is why the beauty of the great epics as well as the simple piercing beauty of the Celtic folk-songs and music connected with death and burial have the power not simply or primarily of expressing sadness but of bringing with them the sense of a peace and a presence beyond death.

V

The belief or intimation of a life beyond death was part of the Celtic vision of life and death long before Christianity came to the Isles of the North and the wide-ranging Celtic world. As in the Greek world of Homer and Plato it was accepted that the dead lived on either in homeric shadowlands or platonic fields of light. The Celtic feeling for life and death tended towards the platonic model with its corollary of many incarnations of the same spirit. However, it was more ready than was the Greek world (as witness St. Paul's experience at Athens in Acts, 17) for the central Christian doctrine of the bodily resurrection or awakening of the human composite of body and soul from the dead. For, as we have seen several times in the course of our incursions into the world of the Celtic imagination (see especially chapter 2, section 4 above), the Celtic peoples shared with much of the ancient pre-Christian world a belief in the kind of perception that was neither sense-perception nor intellectual intuition but rather that which alone can bind both together, the kind of use of imagination which does not only range freely as fantasy or fancy but delicately discovers its own special intermediate world of 'imaginal' reality, at once physical like the world of common perception only more 'subtle', and also hidden and incorruptible like the world of 'pure' spirit or intelligible reality in the platonic sense as commonly understood. Most of what has been said in the foregoing pages is by way of giving body and intimational luminousness to this way of perceiving. it cannot nor should it be brought under any 'scientific' light or microscope, nor should it be dressed up in scientific garments, as some parapsychologists try to dress it. It is seen in a personal way, by the whole person or not at all, and only thus can it be shared with others, with modesty and sensitivity. It was in this way that the people of the Western Isles of Scotland met Alexander Carmichael. It was thus that Barbara McPhie at Dreimsdale 'saw' the sun dancing marvellously at Easter, a reality given to her 'once and only once in her long life' (see chapter 2, Section 3 above).

It is only in the light of this kind of perception that we can make sense of St. Paul's descriptions of the 'awakened' or resurrected body as a 'spiritual' body.[42] The 'spiritual body' of St. Paul can be understood in terms of imaginal reality and the

---

[42]See N. D. O'Donoghue, 'The Awakening of the Dead' in *The Irish Theological Quarterly* Jan. 1990 for a fuller discussion of the Christian doctrine of the resurrection of the body.

physical-incorruptible; otherwise it becomes a metaphor merely. One of the reasons why the Christian message of bodily resurrection through Christ was easily acceptable to the Celtic mind was that this mind already possessed the category to deal with it, as also to deal with the angelic realm so much in evidence in the Christian gospel. If we are to recover that first Christian vision in its purity and delicacy we have to try to make in our day a living connection with that Celtic vision of another world within the everyday world of common perception and the things that pass away, of that 'bright mountain behind the mountain' that gives us intimations of a new heaven and a new earth.

INDEX

Aberdeen, 83, 85, 88
Achilles, 94
Acts of the Apostles, 23
Aeschylus, 94
Alexander, Mrs, 12
Ambrose, 44
America, 58
Angels, 21, 23, 27, 39, 48, 62, 69, 74, 75, 79, 108, 111, 113, 114, 115, 116, 118, 121, 123, 125
   Angelic presences, 40, 61, 75
   Angelic hierarchies, 106
   Angelic regions, 50
   Fallen angels, 108, 109, 112, 119
   Guardian angels, 63, 110
   Spirit world, 27, 62, 106, 113, 117
   Cosmic persons, powers, 108, 118, 123
Ariel, Gabriel, Raphael, Uriel, 106
Anu (Dana), 39
Aquinas, St Thomas, 10, 44, 95, 99, 113, 114, 115
Aristotle, 94
Asceticism, 61
Augustine, St, 10, 24, 44, 56, 95, 97

and glorified body, 22
Auld Lang Syne, 131

Barth, Karl, 99
Barthélemy-Madaule, M., 83 n. 28
Bás Sona (happy death), 66
Bate, John, 81
Beckett, Samuel, 105
Beltane, 39
Benedicite hymn, 13
Berdyaev, Nicholas, 97
Bergonzi, B., 129 n. 38
Betjeman, John, 73
Bittleston, Adam, 16 n. 8
Blake, William, 36
Böll, Heinrich, 73
Bonaventure, St, 44, 99
Brigit, St, 80
Burial chant, 68

Caesar, Julius, 9, 11
Cailleach, 64, 80
Calvary, 104, 124
Canada, 58
Caoine (lament), 57
Carmichael, Alexander, ix, x, 41, 46, 52, 54, 55, 76
Carmina, Gadelica, ix, x, 16, *passim*

Blessing of the Kindling, 62
Consecration of the Seed, 64, 76, 79
Hatching Blessing, 54
Repose Blessing, 50
Celibacy, 122
Chateaubriand, 129 n.38
Chesterton, G. K., 41, 42, 84, 97
Churn-Staff blessing, 78
Celtic consciousness, 2, 58
   Christianity, 15, 82, 113
   Cosmology, 106
   Cross, 3
   Europe, 1
   Folk-songs, 135
   Imagination, 6, 89, 93, 106
   Inner vision, 103, 107, 137
   Mind, 6
   Musical tradition, 58
   Nature world, 12
   Poetry, 37
   Tradition, 30, 35, 37, 46
Clermont-Ferrand, 9, 82, 85, 88
Corbin, Henri, 127 n.37
Creation, 78, 85, 113, Ch.7, *passim*
   King of, 56
   Name that is highest of all, 59
   Created nature, 73, 76
Croagh, Patrick, 7, 34
Crobh Dearg, 20, 41
Cronin, Daniel, 40 n.14
Cuénot, Claude, 83 n.28

Dana, D*á Keek anainn,* 4, 18, 20, 25, 40, 43, 70
   Breasts of, 39, 45, 47, 70
   Paps of, 98
Danes, The, 2
Dante, 92, 97, 99, 113, 121
De Faoite, S., 25
Descartes, 92
Dragon, The Great, 93, 94, 101, 102, 115, 123, 124
Druids, The, 7
Dualism, 51, 67, 108
Duns Scotus, John, 115
Dying Galatian, The, 1

Easter Sunrise, 15, 16
Eckhart, Meister, 92
Eleatics, 95
Eliot, T. S., 33, 57, 62, 125, 129
Elohim, 72
Ember days, 20
Endean, Philip, 44 n. 16
Enoch, 72
Eriugena, Scotus, 11, 103
Eros, 121, 122
Euripides, 94
Evans-Wentz, W. Y., 5 n.3, 66

Fall (of man), 56
Fatima, 39
Ferris, William, 40
Flesk, River, 18, 19
Folk consciousness, 25
   imagination, 21
Funeral (in Lewis), 39

Gaelic languages, ix, 57
Genesis, 86, 97
Genetic manipulation, 115
Gergovie, 9, 20, 88, 103
Gethsemane, 104, 109, 124
Glenstal Abbey, 45

Gnostic Christians, 108
Gormenghast, 85
Graves, A. P., 12
Gray, Donald, 83 n. 28
Great Tradition, The, 62

Hardy, Thomas, 17, 32
Hanson, R. P. C., 14 n. 7
Heidegger, Martin, 71, 81
Hell, 61, 107, 112
Hellenistic (Greek) Philosophy, 10, 15, 114
Henry, P. L., 13
Hidden world, (perception of), viii, ix, 18, 42
Highland Clearances, 57
Hopkins, G. M., 57, 61, 133
Hyde, Douglas, 18, 46

I am going home with Thee, 67
Ikon, 45
Imaginal World (mundus imaginalis), viii, 14, 22, 26, 32, 126 n. 37, 128
Imagination, viii, 21, 35, 47, 60, 61, 86, 103
  Light of, 31, 129
  Projective/receptive, viii
  Visionary, 44
  imaginary/imaginal, 32
Immortality, 5, 63
Intimational knowledge, 33, 36
Intentionally, 62
Iona, 2
Irish Famine, 57, 71, 72
Isaiah, 9

Jahweh Sabaoth, 108
Jansenism, 61

Jesus of Nazareth, Jesus Christ, 3, 55, 112, 124
  Nativity, 123
  Passion and death, 71
  Mediator, 112
  King of Friday, 79
  Crucifixion, 127
  Resurrection, 9, 23, 35, 79, 101, 109, 112, 123, 124
  Ascension, 35, 63, 101
  Redeemer, 53, 72, 113
John the Baptist, St, (Midsummer Bonfire), 19
John of the Cross, St, 36, 51, 101
Joyce, James, 105
Jung, C. G., 43, 126 n. 37

Kavanagh, Patrick, 3
Kennedy-Fraser, M., 6
'Keening' the dead, 67, 126
'Kindling' of fire, 47, 48
Kinsella, P., 131 n. 40, 133, 133 n. 41
Knock Shrine, 39

Lamma Sabachthani, 101
Leannann Shee (Fairy Folk), 5, 22, 24, 43, 66, 70, 128
Lewis, C. S., ix, 32, 86
Life-entelechies, 27
Lilliput, 86
Liturgy, 73, 78
  Domestic, 50, 76, 119
  Angelic, 112
  Eucharistic, 119
Lochnagar, 25
Logos, 72
Love of Learning, 6
Lourdes, 39

Lugh, 9
Lyons, J. A., 83 n. 28

Mackey, J. P., 74 n. 25
Mananaan, 9
Mangan, J. C., 12
Marcel, Gabriel, 97
Martin, Robert B., 61 n. 22
Mary, Mother of Jesus, 35, 39, 41, 42, 43, 44, 80, 101
  Mary of Mount Carmel, 28
  Mary of Walsingham, 43
  Marian Shrine, 20
  Marian Piety, 45
  In Praise of Mary, 65
  Seven Sorrows of Mary, 71
  Mary's Son, 40, 42, 80, 124
Materia Coelestis, 134
Medawar, P. B., 104
Memoria Dei, x, 134
Memory, 126
Michael, Archangel, 77, 106
Midsummer Christmas, 27
Monod, Jacques, 104
Moore, Thomas, 120

MacDonald, George, 31, 32, 83, 84, 85, 103, 105
MacNeill, Maire, 40 n. 14
MacPhie, Barbara, 16, 136
McKenzie, Agnes Muir, 68
McIntyre, John, 84
McLean, G. R. D., 16 n. 8
McLean, Sorley, 57

Nature, 38, 53, 56
  Voice of, 37
  Unity with, 4, 15, 50
  Worship of, 13
Neoplatonism, 49, 108

New Testament, 10, 35, 36, 38, 51, 93, 108, 110, 112, 113, 119, 123, 127
Nicene Creed, 27
Nietzsche, F., 128
'Northernness', xii
Nuclear Pysics, 115

O'Rahilly, Aogan, 132, 133
Origen, 118
O'Riordan, Sean, 57
Old Testament, 10, 38, 108

Paganism, 8
Parousia, 106
Pathos, 8, 9, 57, 126
Patrick, St, 7, 8
  St Patrick's Breastplate, 12, 38, 64, 73, 74, 75, 76, 79
Paul, St, 20, 53, 118, 136
Pernoud, R., 88 n. 30
Physical Sky (as interface), 110
Plato, 10, 94, 135
Plotinus, 30, 37, 49, 92, 95, 134
Poulain, P., 44 n. 16
Powers, Jessica, ix
Prayer, 48, 49, 50, 61, 64, 73, 121, 123, 124, 125
Presence, presences, 22, 31, 32, 34, 36, 37, 48, 61
Presence of God, 52, 54, 56, 59 n. 21
Privatio (*steresis*), 95
Proust, Marcel, 128 n. 38

Rahner, Karl, 26
Raine, Kathleen, 5 n. 3, 23, 29, 34, 51, 104, 127 n. 37
Reformation, Ministers of, 60

Rhythms of life, 57, 58
Rideau, Émile, 83 n. 28
Ritual, 54
Roman influence, 11, 15

Sacred Space, 67
Sarcenat, 67
Satan (adversary), 63, 80, 93, 120
 see Angels (Fallen)
Scottish Calvinism, 84
Seven Wonders of the World, xiii
Shaw, G. B., 105
Sheila-na-gig, 80
Slane, Hill of, 7, 9
Smooring (of fire), 47
Speaight, Robert, 83 n. 28
Spirit of God, 124
Spiritual Body, 53, 136
Steiner, Rudolph, 5, 66, 126 n. 37
Streit, Jacob, 3 n. 2
Spiritual Senses, 44, 45
Suffering Servant, 9
Sun Worship, 13
Supersitition, 59 n. 21

Teilhard de Chardin, Pierre, x, 20, 82, 85, 89, 103, 104, 105, 106, 125
 Teilhardism, x, 72
 Complexity-consciousness, 89, 100, 106
 Cosmogenesis, 82, 88, 89, 91, 100, 116
 Christogenesis, 116, 118
 Point Omega, 89, 91, 100, 116
 Radial energy, 89, 100, 117

'Union Differentiates', 90, 116
Le Christique, 101, 107
Le Milieu Divin, 96
The Phenomenon of Man, 96
Turmoil or Genesis, 107
Temenos, 127 n. 37
Teresa of Avila, 57, 99
Terra Viventium, 111
Tolkien, J. R. R., 32, 86

Ulysses, 94
Urbanisation, 115

Vatican II, 102
Vercingetorix, x, 9, 88

Warnock, Mary, 43, 128 n. 38
Weitz, Morris, 128 n. 38
Winckelmans de Cléty, Charles, 118
Wodehouse, P. G., 32
Wordsworth, William, 5, 33, 61, 92, 100, 134

Yeats, W. B., 34, 57, 66